Freedom
Is Never
Free

Freedom Is Never Free

Richard A. Jackson

BROADMAN PRESS
Nashville, Tennessee

ISBN: 0-8054-1936-5
4219-36

Dewey Decimal Classification: 252
Subject headings: SERMONS//PATRIOTISM-SERMONS

Library of Congress Catalog Card Number: 75-42861
Printed in the United States of America

Dedicated to my family
Don, Doug, Tena, and their mother, Wanda,
who is inspiration to us all—

—and to our larger family,
The fellowship of believers in the
North Phoenix Baptist Church
Phoenix, Arizona

Contents

Preface

1776–1976
    America
        Freedom
            Jesus Christ
                Religious Liberty
                    Bible
                        Baptists
                            Preaching

These words, like ham and eggs, ice cream and apple pie, hot dogs and mustard, hit and run, ball and glove just seem to go together. They are words which represent principles. They are words which represent our loftiest ideals. They are words that identify a people. They are words which speak a message. They are words we cherish. You are about to read a book that dynamically expresses something of the magnitude of these mighty words.

A preacher by the name of Richard Jackson has taken this significant period in our history to make an excellent contribution in the field of evangelistic preaching with a patriotic theme. I met Richard at a seminar in which we had parts on the program. He was to share some insights into the miraclulous growth of the North Phoenix Baptist Church where he serves as pastor. Instead he changed the subject and preached to preachers. Up one side and down the other, he peeled ecclesiastical skins. He took us to task for two traits that show up all too often in the ministry—jealousy and laziness. He concluded by pouring the oil of challenge and the balm of love on our wounded hides. He got his point across, and his fiery enthusiasm for Christ and his church left no one in doubt as to why his church was growing. That was the way I met him. Since then our paths have crossed often. I've followed his Spirit-anointed ministry very closely. His church stands among the best of Southern Baptist churches. Year after year it is among the leaders in conversions and baptisms, most of these being adults. Richard preaches three times every Sunday morning to capacity crowds as well as to a large, widespread television audience. In the far west he has led his faithful congregation to build a great spiritual church in an area where many said it would be unlikely and nearly impossible to achieve.

Richard lives what he preaches. He witnesses consistently of our Lord's love and grace in the normal flight patterns of daily living. This book of expository sermons reflects his intense love for the Savior, the Bible, the church, the people, and the nation. You will feel the evangelistic thrust that underscores all of his preaching. You will know you are reading a man who has been set free and desires spiritual and national freedom for all people. You will see in the man The Man who makes it all possible, and you will realize anew that freedom is never free, for we are "bought with a price." That price has never been rescinded spiritually or nationally . . . and never will be.

Jim Henry

Two Rivers Baptist Church
Nashville, Tennessee

Revelation 5:1-10

And I saw in the right hand of him that sat on the throne a book written within and on the backside sealed with seven seals.

And I saw a strong angel proclaiming with a loud voice, Who is worthy to open the book, and to loose the seals thereof?

And no man in heaven, nor in earth, neither under the earth, was able to open the book, neither to look thereon.

And I wept much, because no man was found worthy to open and to read the book, neither to look thereon.

And one of the elders saith unto me, Weep not: behold the Lion of the tribe of Juda, the root of David hath prevailed to open the book, and to loose the seven seals thereof.

And I beheld, and lo, in the midst of the throne, and of the four beasts, and in the midst of the elders, stood a Lamb as it had been slain, having seven horns and seven eyes, which are the seven Spirits of God sent forth into all the earth.

And he came and took the book out of the right hand of him that sat upon the throne.

And when he had taken the book, the four beasts and four and twenty elders fell down before the Lamb having every one of them harps and golden vials full of odours, which are the prayers of saints.

And they sung a new song, saying, Thou art worthy to take the book, and to open the seals thereof: for thou wast slain, and hast redeemed us to God by thy blood.

And has made us unto our God kings and priests: and we shall reign on the earth.

1
Freedom Is Never Free

The young man stood straight as he walked across the platform to the pulpit of our church. There was a patch where his left eye should have been. A hook extended from the artificial limb where a strong left arm had once helped make him an outstanding athlete. His face had been repaired through the process of more than two dozen operations. Through it all the former college athlete, high school coach, and young family man had a certain handsome appearance which drew admiration from all the congregation.

Lieutenant Clebe McClary went on to share his story. At twenty-six years of age he had left his coaching career to enlist in the United States Marine Corps. Following training in Quantico, he had been sent to Vietnam. While leading his nineteenth "recon" patrol, Clebe and his twelve men were attacked. Two gave their lives; four others were severely wounded. The handsome young man from Georgetown, South Carolina, was miraculously lifted to safety by helicopters, along with the wounded and survivors of the attack.

On a plaque presented to Lt. McClary by his admiring men is the statement, "In this world of give and take, there

are all too few who are willing to give what it takes."
Surely, Clebe McClary is an example to us that freedom is
never free. It is always bought with blood. Down through
the years it has ever been so. This young man came home
to learn of his personal need for Christ and accept him as
Lord and Savior. He lives to tell the story that many left
untold in a bath of death's bloody battles.

As I listened to that testimony, I prayed again, "Oh,
Lord God, somehow we need to remind Americans of the
price our freedom has cost." Those who are guilty of de-
facing the flag, of criticizing and never helping, of taking
and never giving need to know how to appreciate that
freedom for which such a price has been paid. Surely, we
should know that freedom is never free. It is purchased by
those who are willing to "give what it takes."

Freedom is never free. This significantly important
principle was clearly at work during those painful years in
the mid—1700's when the old order was giving way to the
new, when the time of separation was near. Beloved pa-
triots such as John Adams understood the cost of liberty.
On July 4, 1776, the day the Declaration of Independence
was formally adopted and signed, Adams said in an address
before the Continental Congress: "Live or die; sink or
swim; survive or perish; I am committed to this Declaration
of Independence. I am committed, and if God wills it, I
am ready to die that this nation may be free." Because of
that declaration, men equipped with little more than hunt-
ing rifles went out to do battle with the greatest nation in
the world in that day. By human valor and sacrifice, they
won the freedom we enjoy. Freedom is never free; it is
bought by blood.

The errant ways of men had capitalized upon the slavery

system of the South by 1861. Citizens had concocted a method through which freedoms in the land were extended to some but not to all. Following years of sectional strife, President Abraham Lincoln signed the Emancipation Proclamation to set the slaves free. The result was a bloody civil war. Soon, father fought against son; brother against brother. A scarred trail of blood and devastation was carved all over this nation because freedom had been threatened. The cost to the nation was best expressed in a letter written by President Lincoln to a Mrs. Bixby of Boston. He said:

> I have been shown in the files of the War Department a statement of the Adjutant General of Massachusetts that you are the mother of five sons who died gloriously on the field of battle. I feel how weak and fruitless must be any word of mine which should attempt to beguile you from the grief of a loss so overwhelming. But I cannot refrain from tendering you the consolation that may be found in the thanks of the republic they died to save. I pray that our Heavenly Father may assuage the anguish of your bereavement, and leave you only the cherished memory of the loved and lost, and the solemn pride that must be yours to have laid so costly a sacrifice upon the altar of freedom.

That mother who lost her five sons would cry out to us down through the ages of time: "Freedom is never free; it is blood bought."

When World War I broke out in Europe in 1914, people in the United States thought they could rest in safety three thousand miles from battle, but soon United States' ships were attacked on the high seas by German submarines. President Woodrow Wilson said, "This is an attack on mankind, this is warfare." War was declared and more than one hundred thousand men died of disease and wounds from that great world holocaust. Freedom is never free; it is blood bought.

World War II came, and it would seem once again that the United States would try to stay at home but such was not to be. In December, 1941, Japan launched her infamous attack upon Pearl Harbor. Men died by the thousands. Equipment and a large portion of America's Pacific Fleet was wiped out. On December 8, 1941, Congress approved a declaration of war with only one dissenting vote. The United States was again thrust into a conflict to preserve freedom and to share it with freedom-loving people in the world.

One dear lady who is a faithful member of our church left three of her five sons on those fields of battle. Mrs. Bess Schwensen could say to you today: "Freedom is never free, people; it is bought by blood—blood of our sons who died that we might be free."

In more recent days, we've been given the gory details regarding American men who are persecuted in the prisons of the Vietcong. With them we say: "Freedom is never free; it is always blood bought." My prayer to God is that the people who say, "better Red than dead"—the people who enjoy the privileges that have been won for us—the people who sew the flag on the seat of their pants—might hear sweet Bess Schwensen say: "Freedom is never free; it is blood bought."

There is, however, no clearer illustration of the price of freedom than that seen in the purchase of man from spiri-

tual bondage. The apostle Paul spoke of it in Romans and
Galatians. He said that we have been made free in Christ
"from the law of sin and death." Man's severest struggle is
against sin's binding power. The bondage most difficult to
break is the bondage of Satan and sin. When God devised
the way to loose man from bondage, the plan was neither
free nor easy. It exacted from God a great price. God decreed that sin brings death. Only one who was sinless could
atone for others. God must send his own Son. How would
he be presented? Not as a ruler to enslave, but as a lamb of
sacrifice to die. Freedom is never free. Spiritual freedom
is not free. It is bought. It is purchased in the blood of the
Lord Jesus Christ.

Looking ahead to future events with John, the writer of
Revelation, we see in chapter 5 the King of glory sitting on
his throne, holding in his hand the documents pertaining to
man's eternal redemption. In the King's hands is a book
that is sealed shut. John tells of a search throughout
heaven for one who is able to open that scroll and offer to
man ultimate redemption. Heaven was searched, along
with the earth and the regions underneath the earth, and
no one was found worthy to open the seal.

John began weeping in distress. Then one of the elders
who represents all of the redeemed of all ages said not to
weep, for "the Lion of the tribe of Juda" is to come and
open the book of redemption. John looked, expecting to
see a lion. Instead, he saw a lamb, as if it had been slain.

This can refer to no one other than Jesus Christ our
Lord, the Lamb of God who takes away the sin of the
world; the one who died on Calvary that we might live
unto God. Jesus was dead and is alive forevermore. He
alone offers redemption. He only, offers freedom from sin.

But, my dear friend, let me remind you, freedom is never free. The cost to God was his Son put to death on Calvary. In response, we hear the redeemed as they all join together and sing, "Worthy is the Lamb who was slain for the sins of men." May the Lord use this Scripture passage to drive home to your heart the fact that freedom from sin, the greatest freedom that a man can know, is not free. It cost God the blood of his Son.

Freedom is bought by God. The Bible says, "Thou didst purchase us unto God." The redemption of man is first of all in the power and in the plan of almighty God. The offer of freedom is meaningful only insofar as the one offering it is capable of fulfilling the offer. If we as people of these United States of America are to remain free, we must follow those procedures that make our nation strong.

Uncertainty clouds the future of America. No democracy such as ours has ever lived more than two hundred years. We have reached our two-hundredth year; who knows what is going to happen to our freedoms. Our freedoms rest in the strength of men, but being freed from sin rests in the strength and the power of God.

The Bible teaches in Ephesians 1 that God has redeemed us by his own choosing; he has saved us in his own elective grace. Do not think for a moment that salvation is a happenstance or afterthought with God. Before time began— before man had been touched by sin—God designed his plan of redemption. The Bible says that Jesus Christ is the Lamb of God, slain from the foundation of the earth. We are not saved by accident. When God planned to redeem man unto himself, he planned to do it by the giving of his Son. Freedom is never free; it is bought by blood.

Freedom from sin is purchased in Christ's sacrifice.

Again we look to the Scripture which says concerning the Lamb, "Thou wast slain and hast redeemed us to God." The Lamb was slain. We are purchased with the blood of Jesus Christ. This can have reference only to the cross and Christ's sacrificial death for us on Calvary.

A memorable experience during a recent tour of Israel came when we visited the place of Jesus' crucifixion. A British scholar by the name of Gordon discovered what has been accepted by most modern archaeologists as Golgotha, the hill on which the Savior was crucified. Many details fit the account in the Gospels. It is a rugged hill, having shapes that suggest the features of a skull. It is located outside the walls of the old city of Jerusalem. At the foot of the hill are some small caves that could easily have served as tombs.

As I stood near that small hill, I had the impulse to say to the crowds of people around me, "Keep still so I can meditate on what happened here." But noise filled the air; noise from talking people, passing automobiles, and a crew of laborers at work nearby. Then I was stricken with a memory: It wasn't quiet here when Jesus died. People were cursing him; people were railing at him; the mob was jeering! Oh, there was noise, noise, noise! As I stood near that hill, I thought, Oh God, lest I ever forget, Jesus Christ purchased my pardon from sin on a cross. Freedom is never free; it is blood bought. Freedom from sin is bought by the precious blood of Jesus our Lord.

Oh, some people want to say we are mistaken when we preach about free salvation by grace. It is too easy that way. It is too cheap. They insist that those who receive it must work for it. The man who believes that salvation by grace is free and, therefore, cheap does not understand what happened on Calvary. For Jesus Christ extended himself on a cruel cross between heaven and earth with nails through his hands; a spear was thrust in his side; a crown of thorns placed on his brow. With his body bloody and aching, he hung there and died. I say to you, that is not cheap! That is not small!

When God would free man from sin, he gave the best that heaven had to offer. He bankrupted glory for man to be saved. Freedom is not free; salvation is not free. It cost God the blood of Jesus. He gave "his life a ransom for many," Mark said. He "gave himself a ransom for all," Paul said to Timothy. To the Galatians he wrote that Christ "redeemed us from the curse of the law." In 1 Corinthians Paul wrote, "Ye are bought with a price." The death of Jesus Christ was the cost of man's freedom from sin.

Freedom, to be genuine, is freedom without limit. All of the other freedoms of man have limitations. Such as slavery was before the Civil War in America, so men are today. Impoverished by spiritual darkness and ignorance, they are not free as they could be. Any freedom man has ever had is limited, but the freedom from sin through Christ Jesus is without limit. That freedom is offered to everyone—to all who will call upon him. The grace of God through Christ is not limited to any race or nation. It is for everyone. Isaiah rings with the message, "Ho, every one that thirsteth . . . come ye, buy, and eat . . . without money and without price." Jesus said to all men, "Behold, I stand at the door, and knock: if any man hear my voice, and open the door, I will come in to him" (Rev. 3:20). And again we read, "Whosoever will, let him come." Oh, the freedom of God in Christ from sin is freely available because Jesus purchased it in his blood. It is available to all men who will by faith commit themselves unto Jesus and receive him as Lord.

The urge for freedom often motivates the establishing of new groupings of men. When American pioneers sought freedom, they established a new nation, the United States of America; when Christ came to redeem us from sin, he established his kingdom. Our text says, "And hast made us unto our God kings and priests: and we shall reign on the earth." As men partake of Christ's redemption, they become new citizens in God's kingdom—priests to minister to this world, and princes to reign with him in the next world. The passage in Revelation 5 points to a sequence of future events. Here are some things we can look forward to: God has, in Christ, made us a nation to reign for eternity. When Jesus comes again, all of those who have found freedom from sin through his sacrifice shall reign with him for all eternity. He has made us a kingdom unto God forever and ever.

Freedom is never free. If you would be free, you must pay a price. Those who have gone before you left a legacy of freedom. You must pay the price to claim it for yourself. We, as Americans, have claimed that inheritance and therefore must keep a constant vigil ere it slip away. My dear friend, Christ—God's worthy Lamb—was slain to purchase true freedom for you and for me. The way we claim that freedom is to take hands off our lives, put them in the hands of the Lord Jesus, and say to the Lamb who was slain for our sin: "Worthy art thou, oh Lord to receive honor and praise and glory forever and forever."

'Tis the church triumphant singing,
 Worthy is the Lamb.
Heaven throughout with praises singing,
 Worthy is the Lamb.
Thrones and powers before Him bending,
 Incense sweet and voice ascending,
Swell the chorus never ending,
 Worthy is the Lamb.

Every kindred, tongue and nation,
 Worthy is the Lamb.
Join to sing the great salvation,
 Worthy is the Lamb.
Land as mighty thunder roaring,
 Floods of mighty waters pouring
Prostrate at His feet adoring
 Worthy is the Lamb.

Harp and songs forever sounding,
 Worthy is the Lamb.
Mighty grace o'er sin abounding,
 Worthy is the Lamb.
By His blood He dearly bought us.
 Wandering from the fold He sought us,
And to glory faithful brought us,
 Worthy is the Lamb.

Sing with what anticipation
Worthy is the Lamb.
Through the veil and tribulation,
Worthy is the Lamb.
Sweetest note, all notes excelling
On the throne forever dwelling
Still untold, though ever telling
Worthy is the Lamb.

—Author Unknown

Romans 9:18-26

Therefore hath he mercy on whom he will have mercy, and whom he will he hardeneth.

Thou will say then unto me, Why doth he yet find fault? For who hath resisted his will?

Nay but, O man, who art thou that repliest against God? Shall the thing formed say to him that formed it, Why hast thou made me thus?

Hath not the potter power over the clay, of the same lump to make one vessel unto honour, and another unto dishonour?

What if God, willing to shew his wrath, and to make his power known, endured with much longsuffering the vessels of wrath fitted to destruction:

And that he might make known the riches of his glory on the vessels of mercy, which he had afore prepared unto glory,

Even us, whom he hath called, not of the Jews only, but also of the Gentiles?

As he saith also in O see, I will call them my people, which were not my people? and her beloved, which was not beloved.

And it shall come to pass, that in the place where it was said unto them, Ye are not my people; there shall they be called the children of the living God.

2
A Nation in Need

The Congress of the United States proclaimed in April, 1974, a National Day of Humiliation, Prayer, and Fasting. Whatever else this may be, it is at least a recognition that ours is a nation in need.

Evidence abounds on every hand to prove to us that this is true. We are crippled by crime and corruption from the White House to the smallest hovel. Our economy is shaky and threatening to collapse. Violence is rampant in every city and hamlet throughout the land. Moral standards have become meaningless while men indulge themselves to the discount of all that God calls decent and holy.

One out of every three marriages in our land is broken asunder. Children who expected so much from their heroes—Mom and Dad—are standing by watching these lives crumble around them while men give themselves to a deluge of depravity. Ours is indeed a nation in need.

While we as Christians rejoice in this momentary awareness on the part of our Congress, there is corruption in our land which can be controlled only by divine intervention. Perhaps our leaders may listen to the Scripture that declares: "Righteousness exalteth a nation; but sin is a reproach to any people." We need to recognize that no temporary, passing, momentary patchwork is going to provide the answer to the need of this or any other nation.

We need to come to grips with reality. Rather than surveying the symptoms on the circumference and never getting to the heart of the matter of sin in our land, we need to find what our nation's need is and to understand that need at its real core. The need of a nation is actually nothing more than the summation of the needs of individuals within that nation. The sin of a nation is simply the multiplicity of the sins of the people who make up that nation. Whatever else is true, it is truc that the reality in a person is that which becomes the reality in persons who are put together. The United States of America, the nation we call home, the land that we so love, is simply a combination of those things which exist in your life and in mine.

As we view our nation, we see the nation of Israel in the text of Scripture, and we find application to our land in this crucial day. We would do well to consider these Scriptures in light of our personal need. It is only as individuals find their needs met in a right relationship to God that nations of individuals will find the victory that is the result.

In our text we come to a special section of Romans. Chapters 9, 10, and 11 of Romans are very nationalistic, very sectarian passages of Scripture. After weaving the threads of the tapestry picture of God's salvation for man, the sanctification of man, and man's sin and need in the earlier part of the book, the apostle Paul deals with the gospel as it applies particularly to the nation of Israel. The first eight chapters of Romans are didactical chapters presenting theological truths, the great principles of the gospel. In chapters 9, 10, and 11, the apostle, who was himself a Hebrew of the Hebrews, a trained Jewish theologian with a

burden on his heart and a concern for his kinsmen according to the flesh, comes to deal with the particular application of the Christian gospel to the Jewish people.

Paul recounts the facts dealing with God's exceedingly
great promises to the nation of Israel through their fathers
Abraham, Isaac, Jacob, Moses, David, and Solomon. As
God had spoken to Israel, most of his promises centered
in the Messiah whom the Jews themselves murdered on
Calvary's cross. The apostle Paul was led to inform the
Jewish people that, even though they were responsible for
the death of Jesus, God, in his great love, would give them
another opportunity. Individual Israelites, individual Jews,
as well as we who are Gentiles, can be saved even from the
guilt of his death and our own sin by faith in Jesus Christ,
by accepting him. The book of Acts is a record of God's
offering to Israel and to all men an opportunity for that
second chance.

Paul goes further as he comes to grips with the reality
that the majority of Jewish people had upheld the original
verdict of those who crucified Jesus and had rejected him
as their Savior. Having declared that serious indictment,
Paul leads us to see that these in the homeland of Israel and
those of the dispersion, Jews all over the world, had rejected
Jesus Christ. So it is his burden, his prayer, his deep concern that they might see the error of their way and come
to live through faith and belief in Christ.

When Paul wrote the letter to the Romans, the Temple
was still standing in Jerusalem. The sacrifices were being
offered, and the ritual was relentlessly pursued. The
shadows of the nation's fate had not yet darkened the ho-
rizon. The apostle knew that Judaism in the form he knew
it was coming to an end. He knew that the old order had

already been replaced by the new covenant of faith in Jesus Christ. He also knew that the nation of Israel would not stand long. He received the impression from God's Holy Spirit that a tremendous calamity was coming. So Paul, with a burden on his heart for Israel, both spiritually and nationalistically, writes in these chapters his concern for the people of Israel.

In chapter 9 he deals with the key to God's past dealings with Israel: it is the sovereignty of God. He reminded his Jewish brothers that God had dealt with them in the past according to his sovereignty. In chapter 10 he talks about the present dealings with the Israelites. God deals with them by offering salvation. In chapter 11, he writes about the future of God's dealing with Israel, the key of which is the sincerity of God.

For our particular application, we consider how Paul talks about God's dealings with the nation Israel. We can see the sovereign hand of God at work in a nation. You and I can find here in this nationalistic message to Israel a picture of America and her need for spiritual renewal. There are some things I want to point out in what can be only a brief survey of this Scripture passage.

We of thinking of the need of a nation, thinking of the basics which a people must have. If we truly are going to be concerned about the need of our nation, we must come to the place where we have, first of all, an anguish over America's sin. In the first three verses of this chapter, Paul speaks of the anguish of his heart for the people of Israel. Here he grapples with more than a mere academic problem; he grapples with one which has deeply and emotionally involved all there is in him. The situation is one which has wrung out Paul's heart in the deepest, bitterest agony. He is saying to his people: "I have come to speak to you, my kinsmen—my brethren—out of a soul of love, out of a heart of anguish; I am concerned for Israel that she might be saved."

There is no use for you—for me—to say that we are concerned about the United States of America. there is no need for us to have a National Day of Humiliation, Prayer, and Fasting, unless we can get to the place where we have an anguish in our souls over the sin in our nation. So long as you and I can excuse sin in our own lives, we will turn our head away from sin in the lives of others. So long as we have no anguish in our heart when we have failed God, we will have no anguish over the sin of our nation.

If we are to come to grips with America's need, we must recognize that the land is wracked with sin, crime, and violence. All this creates a point of rebellion against God, and the result of that rebellion follows. If we are going to see anything done about it, then we must come to days of prayer, fasting, and humiliation, days of repentance because of godly sorrow in our hearts over the sin of our own soul and the sin of the people of America.

Observe some things in our text. Paul feels an anguish that is born in a heart of love. The apostle said, "I say the truth, I lie not." Paul loved the people of Israel. The Jews had beaten him, they had imprisoned him, they had cursed him and castigated him, and some believers had sought to bring his gospel of grace into disrepute by adding Jewish ritual to the Christian gospel. Yet Paul loved them and longed for them to come to Christ. Such love is not natural. That kind of love is the work of the Spirit. Here, is a man who loved people who were not lovely to him.

We Christians, those of us who know God, those of

us who would be used of God effectively to make a change in America, must somehow reach the point at which we can love Americans, those on the street, those with whom we disagree. We must learn to love them in a supernatural manner that is explained only in the Spirit of God. That kind of love is stronger than death. It is longer than life. It is the sort of love spoken about in 1 Corinthians 13. It is the love that is shed abroad in our hearts by the Holy Spirit. It is the love that brought God's Son from the highest heaven to die in agony, blood, and shame on a cruel Roman cross. As you and I view our nation, let's ask God first of all to give us anguish over America's sin that is born of a love for our country, a concern spiritually. Ask God to help us love our nation beyond her flag, beyond her symbols, beyond her signs. Let us ask God to make us love America because we love Americans, because we are concerned about people, because we are involved with souls, because we want to see men saved.

Paul moves on and shows that his anguish is bolstered by the witness of the Spirit. He doesn't expect people to believe him. Paul uses superlatives here when he says, "I could wish myself accursed for the gospel." He doesn't expect them to believe, therefore, he says, "The Holy Spirit knows I'm not lying." Paul calls on the Spirit to witness to his heart. Only by the witness of the Spirit within us are we going to be, heart and soul, involved in the needs of others around about us.

Notice Paul's anguish brought a willingness to sacrifice. The apostle said, "I could wish myself anathema." The word used here does not mean simply excommunicated from the gospel. To be excommunicated means to be put outside. Paul went much further than that. He says, "I could wish myself assigned unto perdition, devoted unto hell, I would be willing to spend eternity in hell, if Israel could be saved."

We and our congressmen can talk all we want to about being concerned about this nation, but just how much do we care about America? How much are we willing to sacrifice that this nation might be straightened out? Most of us are not really willing to sacrifice. We want to talk about America being straight; we want to talk about America repenting; we want to talk about America coming back to God. But have we reached the place where there is sufficient anguish in our hearts that we say, "God, I am ready to be offered, to be used any way you want to use me that this nation might have her need met in you."

Just how much do you care? Well, don't tell me you care like Paul did. I don't understand this language. I don't understand: "God I am ready to go to hell if my country can be saved." But I would like to understand it. There must be on my heart a burden that's close to Paul's so that I could say: "Oh, God, use me, use mine, use all that I have, take anything out of my life that would prevent my country's repentance. God bring America to Jesus and away from her sin."

The second thing we need is the acknowledgment of America's stewardship. Verses 4-29 are beautiful verses. They say much about the sovereignty of God and the responsibility of those whom God chooses. Responsibility is always born of privilege. As Paul looked into the problem of the Jewish rejection of the Messiah, he saw that the Jewish people, having been especially chosen by God, were particularly responsible to God. She was a nation of privilege and a nation, therefore, of special responsibility.

As we examine the application of these verses to Israel, we would have to be more than stone-blind to miss the application to the United States of America. As you read these verses, you will discover this to be a stewardship arising from God's grace. In verses 4-5 God says to the people of Israel that he chose them and he did it on purpose. In essence, he told them: "God has given you so much but you still will not listen to him. He took you as his own special people, led you along with a bright cloud of glory, and told you how much he wanted to bless you. He gave you his rules for daily life so that you would know what he wanted you to do. He received your worship and gave you mighty promises. Great men of God were your fathers and Christ himself was one of you, a Jew so far as his human nature is concerned—he who now rules over all things. Praise God forever.

You see, Paul advises the Jews that, in the grace of God, they have been given many privileges: adoption as the chosen people; the Shekinah cloud of glory from God; the covenants of Abraham, Moses, and David; and now, the new covenant of Christ. They have been given service and worship activities. Theirs were the great messianic promises. The patriarchs and the other Jewish worthies had provided for them a great heritage.

Paul says that, as great as these privileges were, the one which eclipsed all else was the coming of Christ. Listen to what Paul says about Jesus as related to the Jewish people. He says that Jesus was born of a Jewish mother and reared in a Hebrew home. He attended a Jewish synagogue and was given a Jewish education. He lived and labored in the promised land ministering to the lost sheep of Israel. He came unto his own but, alas, his own received him not. In

the words of Isaiah the prophet, "He is singing to his beloved the song of the vineyard but the grapes of Israel were
wild."

What is Paul saying? He is declaring that God in his
grace has especially chosen to bless Israel. The ultimate in
all those blessings is that he sent Jesus. Yet they rejected
him. Oh, what a parallel runs with America's privilege. We
are a people blessed with a birth that was spiritual. We are
a nation visited by prophets that were powerful. From the
beginning of this nation, preachers of the word of God
have dotted every inch on her map. The gospel of God has
been alive in America. We are a country sealed with a
safety that has been sure, and no foreign power has ever
brought war upon our shores. Our minerals, our natural
resources have been rich indeed. We cannot deny that God
in his grace has abundantly blessed this country.

Abundant blessing and privilege brings abundant responsibility. Therefore, we, as Americans, are more responsible
unto God than other nations less blessed. Even as Israel
was more responsible, so are we more responsible as we
stand before God.

Our stewardship not only comes from God's grace but
we also have a stewardship responsibility as a nation that
extends from God's government. If you will notice verse 6
and the following verses, you will find that while Paul was
impressed with God's gracious dealings with Israel in the
past, he was just as impressed with God's governmental
dealings with them. Paul understood clearly that God's
grace is never administered at the expense of government
and that God's dealings with Israel had always been in keeping with his will and his word. There is nothing capricious
about God's ways. He is not some indulgent grandad who

permits you to do anything you want to do.

I'm reminded of an experience when our minister of music and I entertained members of his family at the motel where we were staying during a revival. A couple—obviously quite intoxicated—came out of the bar and sat at a patio table near where we were seated. Their behavior was most disgusting. The wife especially was loud and offensive in her conversation. After a bit, she grew quiet and then she muttered: "I'm so bored, I'm so bored." And I said: "Lady, we have been to church tonight; we are stone cold sober, and we are not bored." Her response was immediately different: "Oh, yes, isn't God wonderful, and God blesses me and God blesses my husband. My pastor says it doesn't make any difference what you do, what counts is what God does. God just keeps on holding your hand and keeps on blessing you." I said: "Lady, God loves you but you'd better get it out of your head that God is some indulgent old granddaddy somewhere who overlooks your sin. He is going to deal with it in judgment."

Too many people have the idea that because God has chosen America in his grace, he is not going to work in government in America. Do not deceive yourself. God's ways have fixed and righteous guides, and he always follows those righteous guides. What are these guides? Verses 6-13 teach us that they are his superlative wisdom. First of all, he says that God has chosen to bless some and he has done it in his wisdom. Paul says that not everyone born into a Jewish family is Jewish. He says you are not children of Abraham just because you are born of Abraham's seed. To be truly Jewish, to be spiritual Israel, you have to put yourself in line with the works of God. He shows how God in his sovereignty has chosen some and left others in his

wisdom. Jacob and Esau are given as examples along with
Isaac and Ishmael. If you will study these passages closely,
you will find that before Isaac was ever born, God chose
him over Ishmael. Before Jacob and Esau were born, God
said, "I will bless the younger instead of the older of the
twins."

Someone would say that God is unfair in choosing one
and not another. Why? In the first place, none of us deserves anything from God except death and hell. That is
all we deserve. When God in his grace chooses someone, He
does it in keeping with his wisdom. If you review the history
of Ishmael, you will find that he is the father of the Arabs
who were the enemies of God's work and of God's people.
If you will study the record of Esau, you will find that he
is the father of the Edomites who were also the enemies of
God's people. God in his wisdom knew the kind of people
with whom he was dealing, and God knows whom he
chooses. God chose to perform a work in America because
he had knowledge of what America was going to stand for.
When that knowledge indicates to God that America is no
longer useful to him, then his choice will be another people.

In verses 14-24 we find that our stewardship comes from
the government of God which is expressed in his sovereign
will. Notice especially verses 14-15. Paul says that he
imagines some objector would say to him. "But God is
being unfair. You say God chose Israel, and he didn't choose
someone else, then God is being unfair." Listen to what
Paul said: Was God being unfair? Of course not. For God
had said to Moses, 'If I want to be kind to someone, I will.
And I will take pity on anyone I want to.' And so God's
blessings are not given just because someone decides to
have them or works hard to get them. They are given be-

cause God. takes pity on those he wants to."

I know some people have a problem with the sovereignty of God, but we need to get to the place where we understand that God is God. God does what is right. Simply because he is God, what he does is always right and just. His actions are not open to question by men who are limited in intelligence and knowledge and whose moral and spiritual capacity are impaired by sin. In this passage of Scripture, the apostle goes on to use as examples Israel contrasted to Pharaoh and other examples to show how God chooses people according to his sovereign will.

In verses 22-24, Paul says, "Some are fitted for destruction." Now it doesn't mean God made them for destruction. Instead, they are the kind of persons who are fitted by their very nature and by their choices for destruction. "On the other hand," he says, "there are some who are prepared unto glory and those who are prepared unto glory are prepared by God's choice of them." God deals with men so that their inbred wickedness will reveal itself in such a way that they become fit objects for punishment. Those who believe, and fear, and trust God will be prepared for glory.

God is sovereign. If there is anything else I want you to find in this message, I want you to find that note—God is God. One of the problems we have had as Christians is our effort to excuse God for what he does and explain what God does. We must reach the point in our thinking as individuals and as a nation that we can believe God is God, that he has chosen this nation, that he has used this nation, and that he is going to do with this nation what he wants. We must line ourselves up under the sovereign hand of God.

Paul concludes the whole argument in verses 25-29 by

showing that the Gentiles are as much an object of God's mercy as the Jews. Their salvation is not an afterthought. He demonstrates here that God's governmental dealings are never at the expense of his love to all men. Our study of this passage brings clearly to light God's ways with men. Through an extended period God waits in long-suffering patience. Then suddenly he acts, making short work of judgment. He followed that pattern when he sent the flood in Noah's time, the judgment and destruction of Sodom and Gomorrah, and the Syrian and Babylonian captivities of Israel. God waited forty years following Calvary to give the Israelites a chance to repent but, when they finally rejected Jesus in A.D. 70, the armies of Vespasian and Titus swept through the land like a flood bringing to an awful end the national life of Israel.

God deals with nations in patience and long-suffering, but when God's patience has come to an end, a flood tide of judgment awaits. Oh America, we need to repent. God has entrusted us with so much. We have failed so miserably. Individual friend, God has given you a chance to hear the gospel. He has put you in a country where churches present Jesus. He has given you every opportunity to receive him. You must not go on rejecting Jesus. You have the stewardship of privilege and if you refuse the blessed gospel of salvation, the hottest part of hell would not be punishment enough for you.

The answer to America's need is America's salvation. We must have an anguish over America's sin. A nation needs to acknowledge her stewardship and the answer comes in a nation's salvation. In the last part of chapter 9, Paul says, "Now you have seen the problem, we acknowledge our responsibility, what can be done?" What can Israel do? What can America do? What does America need? Does she need clean air? Yes! Does she need better bridges? Yes! Does she need more roads? Yes! But none of these things is the answer.

What does America need? What is America's answer? What is Israel's answer? Paul says the answer is in God's salvation. He said to the Jewish people: "You have been looking for the right thing in the wrong place. You have been trying to work yourself into the grace of God, and the Gentiles who weren't even trying heard the gospel and by faith believed and they have been saved."

Oh, America, what does America need? America needs for America to be saved, for Americans to trust Jesus, for Americans to be redeemed from sin. This solution is not in the attempt of works, but by the attainment of faith in the Lord Jesus Christ. When Jesus lives in the hearts of Americans, I'll guarantee you God will meet America's need!

Genesis 35:1-3

And God said unto Jacob, Arise, go up to Bethel, and dwell there: and make there an altar unto God, that appeared unto thee when thou fleddest from the face of Esau thy brother.

Then Jacob said unto his household, and to all that were with him, Put away the strange gods that are among you, and be clean, and change your garments:

Let us arise and go up to Bethel; and I will make there an altar unto God, who answered me in the day of my distress, and was with me in the way which I went.

A Return to Spiritual Reality

"And God said unto Jacob, Arise, go up to Bethel, and dwell there: and make there an altar unto God, that appeared unto thee when thou fleddest from the face of Esau thy brother" (Gen. 35:1).

Emerson once said, "All of history resolves itself into the biography of a few stout and earnest men." The history of our nation has had such a summary.

We live in a time when cynicism has sought to destroy almost every hero and tradition that Americans have ever cherished. Yet no amount of cynicism or ridicule can ever steal away the glory that belongs to the founding fathers of our great nation. Those devoted pioneers left us a legacy that we should revere. They gave us an example of disciplined living to which we desperately need to return. They bequeathed us the heritage of freedom under the law—a gift essential to good government.

Our fathers left us a legacy of social awareness. They developed a keen concern for one another. They were interested in the welfare of every person about them. There is a need in our day to return to a very special awareness of the needs of our fellowman.

The greatest heritage that has been handed to us from

our forefathers is the example of faith. This nation was
built on men who had a deep unswerving religious conviction and a faith toward God. They were men who believed
in Jesus Christ and his kingdom. They found fulfillment in
him. They had purpose in their lives. They had encountered
the living Christ and they knew it without doubt. The en-
nobling result was that our forefathers feared neither mon-
arch nor man, only God.

Because they belonged to God, they had a deep faith
and confidence in themselves. They believed in their own
dignity, and they were confident that their cause was just.
They walked with an uprightness that only fearless and free
men of faith can display. What a difference in our day,
when our leaders hang their heads in shame. Many who
have risen to places of power cannot stand in confidence
because they are not sure their cause is right. Our nation
was not built by such men, but by men who feared God.
They were convinced their cause was right and walked with
head erect, to live or to die for the divine purpose to which
they had committed everything.

Much of our world today believes nothing. Men are
broad-minded and shallow in their living. Agnosticism,
anxiety, emptiness, and meaninglessness—all have gripped
much of our world. Looking around us, we see our youth
searching for meaning and purpose in life in all kinds of un-
disciplined release and rebellion. By contrast to current
conditions, our forefathers stood as shining lights—men
who were not broad-minded and shallow, but were narrow
and deep in their convictions; men who were certain of
their beliefs, unswerving in their loyalty. They were pas-
sionately dedicated to God, whom they trusted and for
whom they were willing even to die.

Today many have shunned as stupid and lofty the high ideals of our nation's founders—the fighters who forged our freedoms. We fancy ourselves enlightened and enlarged far above them. Technological advances have taught us much about life, but we know so little about living. Even if it were possible to imagine our nation's heroes as being un-learned or ignorant, even if their ideals were lofty but meaningless, we recognize that they built the foundation of the greatest nation the world has ever known on those prin-ciples of faith, discipline, and adherence to law. Modern Americans, educated and enlightened, we think, far above our fathers, will surely destroy our country when we dis-card those indispensable principles.

We must reconsider the question of who is wise and who is unwise, who has found purpose in living by faith in God and who has no purpose in living because of a lack of faith in God. Our nation today desperately needs a return to the reality of spiritual matters. We need a walk toward God, a meeting place with the Master, an audience with the Eternal. That is the only answer to man's longing heart. In plain, old, simple terms, America needs to get back to God. Like the nation, individuals also need to get back to God.

"How can it be done?" I point you to our text to show you how it happened in the life of a man who was to be-come the head of a great nation. His father called him Jacob, a name that means deceiver, swindler. Jacob began his life living up to that name. He unfairly bargained for his brother Esau's birthright. To escape Esau's anger, Jacob made a hasty departure from the land of his father and went for an extended visit with his Uncle Laban. On his first night away from home when the young man Jacob was running from his brother, he made a place of rest.

With the stars for his canopy and a stone for a pillow, God appeared to him in a vision. It seemed that the stones were stacked one on another as a ladder extending into the starry heavens above. Up and down the ladder trooped the angels showing that even in the wilderness there was a gateway to God. From the top of that ladder, Jacob heard the voice of the Eternal.

The young man understood from that strange but encouraging dream that there is a gateway to God anywhere in the wilderness, as long as a person has the eyes of faith. When Jacob awoke the next morning, he remembered his dream. He made a vow unto God. He said if God would be with him and protect him wherever he journeyed, he would give to God a tenth of all that came to him. Jacob established a little altar there and called the place Bethel, "house of God."

Quickly Jacob forgot that vow, like so many of us are prone to do. During that moment of communion with God, he made a lofty commitment only to turn away with a resulting anguish of conscience. You and I know that experience well.

Jacob journeyed on to the land of Laban. He met and fell in love with Rachel, the beautiful daughter of his Uncle Laban. By agreement, he labored seven years for Rachel and then he was tricked into accepting her sister, Leah. He labored another seven years for Rachel. During that period, he begat sons and he gathered to himself animals, flocks, and herds. All of this seemed to produce little more than confusion: two wives, two handmaids, children by all of them, and a disagreement with his father-in-law.

The day came when God's angels visited Jacob and said, "God wants you to move out and go back to the land of

your father." So Jacob made plans to leave his father-in-law
and go back to the land of his father. Gathering his family
and his possessions, he began the return journey to his
father's home. As he was making his way, Jacob recalled
the disagreement with his brother, and he was afraid. But
God intervened in what could have been an ugly confronta-
tion, so that, instead of meeting as enemies, Jacob and Esau
met in a joyful reunion. At about the same time, God gave
him a new name. He said: "You will no longer be Jacob,
the swindler; you will henceforth be called Israel, a prince
of God."

One would think Israel, now advanced in years, had
learned to trust God completely and to stop his shrewd
manipulations. But such was not the case. Despite his
costly experience and despite the promise of God concerning Israel's ownership of the land, Israel bought an extra
tract of land which happened to lie near an enemy strong-
hold. Here is the man whom God wanted so much to bless;
yet, because of the lack of faith, he brought another piece
of ground. Within a short span of time, he was in trouble
again. One of his daughters was defiled by a non-Jewish
neighbor—a man tracked down and slain in vengeance by
two of Israel's sons. In anger they also killed many other
people in the area, and we are told that the name of Jacob
was made to stink among the people roundabout.

The angel of God visited Israel again, and God said to
Israel: "Arise now and go back to Bethel. Go back to the
spot where I last did business with you. Go back to the
place where we met. Go back, Israel, and I will renew my
covenant with you."

Jacob was glad to go. He was in trouble and he felt the
need to get away. So he turned his face to go to Bethel.

He said to all in his household—his wife, his family, his servants—"Bury your idols, clean yourselves, change your garments. We will arise and go to Bethel, and I will build an altar there unto the God of Israel." When they arrived, Jacob found himself to be Israel, now a prince of God; and he rejoiced to be once more in communication with the Eternal.

As we learn from Jacob's experience, we see clearly the need of men and of nations to walk with God. When we have walked away from God, the need is strong for us to return to the place of spiritual reality so that we may again experience the blessings of God. I am conscious that some of you at one time came to know God through faith in Jesus Christ. You made a vow of faith to God and yet along the way you left the path of that commitment and are wandering in misery, agony, and sin. Your need is to arise and go back to the place where you were last aware of God's presence. You need to "go back to Bethel," where God can deal with you again.

I am aware also that some of you have never made the decision to follow God. You have never come to Calvary's cross. You have never been cleansed in the blood of Jesus. God wants to do business with you today. He wants to establish communication with you through his Son, Jesus Christ.

I am aware further that we as a nation were founded upon principles of faith and godliness. America, more than ever before, needs desperately to "go back to Bethel." We need to go back to where our forefathers fell on their faces and thanked God for the bounty he had provided. We need to go back to God.

Some simple but fundamental truths must be considered

if our text is to be applied in daily living. First of all, there is reason for the return. Two things were goading Jacob to go back to Bethel. One was a hunger in his own heart. No man lives well, no man lives correctly, no man lives completely, as long as he is separated from God. Jacob was a man who had made a solemn covenant with God. He had known God's presence; he had heard God's voice. Now he was alone, surrounded by people, but alone, separated from God. Jacob shares with us the frequent occasions when we find ourselves alone. We may have people all about us, but if we are not walking with God, we are men alone. Man is made for God. To live apart from God is to be away from our natural way of living. Each one of us and our nation as a whole need to return to God. Unless we are living in a vital relationship with him, we are living far below our potential and far from our intended purpose. You were not made for Satan and sin; you were not made for Satan's pigpens; you were made for God. The man who is away from God is missing much of the potential for which he was created.

The other thing urging Jacob to return was the call of God. Jacob had made a vow to God and God had made a vow to him. Therefore, the Spirit of God was working in Jacob's life. During all the time Jacob was in the land of Laban, God never stopped. God dealt with him continually. God was calling Jacob to God himself.

Let us be thankful that God has never ceased calling America back to himself. With all my soul, I'm convinced that God was involved in the founding of this nation. I believe that God was involved in bringing her to her greatness. That same faith convinces me this nation shall fall unless she humbles herself in repentance and returns to the God who gave her birth. Our nation needs to go back to God, because God is calling her back to himself. You and I as individuals need to go back to God, because he is intervening in our lives.

Oh, that God could speak through me today to show us the plane on which we are living. I pray to God that we might see that we are living out in Shechem, in the place of sin. It is not where God intended for us to live. Oh, that today you could hear the voice of God saying, "Arise and go up to Bethel."

Great and glorious God, today let this be Bethel in my life. I want to return to my God.

> If thou couldst in vision see thyself, the man God
>   meant,
> Thou never more couldst be the man thou art content.

We need to return to spiritual realities because our nature demands it, and because the great God of glory is calling!

Let me move on to say something about the spiritual realities that are to be recovered. What happens when a person goes back to God? What happens when a nation falls to her knees? When Jacob returned to Bethel, he discovered at least five things that may be experienced by all who do as Jacob did.

On returning to God, he found the same divine protection he had known before. Jacob's life, during the days of his disobedience, was in constant peril. He was forced to leave Shechem, in his words, "lest mine enemies gather themselves together against me and slap me." Can you imagine the reassurance welling up in Jacob's heart as he neared Bethel? He was made keenly aware that the terror of God gathered upon the cities near which he passed, and they did not even pursue him. The protecting hand of God is on those who love him and live for him.

We can see in our nation how God's hand of protection has been upon us! How could our ancestors have taken their squirrel guns from over their fireplaces and defeated a great military machine unless God had been involved in that? And yet today, protected as we are with nuclear weapons and well-trained combat forces, we tremble, we fear, we quake, because we are depending upon ourselves! We need to "go back to Bethel." We need to humble ourselves in repentance. We need to go back to God; to be reminded God's protection is there. When you get right with God, do not be troubled by your enemies or the things that harrass you. Go back to God. He will take care of you. John Greenleaf Whittier said:

> I know not where His islands lift
>> Their fronded palms in air;
> I only know I cannot drift
>> Beyond His love and care.

America, we need to return to spiritual reality; we need to bow before God that his protection may be ours.

Please notice also that when Jacob went back to Bethel he found the old pillar he had fashioned thirty years before to commemorate his vision and his vow. What memories those old moss-covered stones must have stirred for Jacob. He had gone back to the place where he had submitted first to God.

In precisely the same way, we as a nation need to return to the pillars of purity and piety that marked our making. Even so we as individuals need to kneel daily in the place of prayer. Many times people say to me, "Pastor, where is the joy that once I knew when first I met the Lord." My firm reply to everyone is, "It is right where you left it when you turned your back on God, when you walked away, when you quit depending upon God and started depending upon yourself." Go back to that old pillar; go back to that place of prayer; go back to that spot where first you bowed and begged Jesus' forgiveness and asked him into your heart. Was it at your mother's knee? Was it in the pastor's study, in your living room, or at the altar of a church? Go back to that pillar of prayer and power, and you'll find God right where he was when last he dealt with you.

Another thing Jacob found at Bethel was the old princeliness. Strange conduct for a prince! One day he was called "the prince of God," and the next day he let God down. How unworthy he was of the title. And how you and I share that shame. We have been called the sons of God. But how unworthy we are so many times! We as a nation, the people of America, once enjoyed the esteem of nations around the world and now people hold us in disgust. We need to turn again to him alone who can make us princes unto God. Let me tell you that when America wears the crown of righteousness before God, she will again wear the crown of princeliness in the world. And mark you well, the state of princeliness will never be ours again until we first return to godliness.

When Jacob went back to Bethel, he found the old promise . It was there that God first promised a blessing for Jacob and his offspring. When he returned, the high prerogatives of his heritage were renewed, and with them came a renewed strength and freshness about it all that was even greater than its first utterance.

Think of the birthright of a child of God. Consider all

that God intended for us as a people and then think of how
far short we have fallen. But how blessed we are that it is
possible for a person and a nation to come back.

You may insist that you have sinned grievously. I'm certain I have and the nation is guilty, too. Is there any hope?
The answer is yes. It is still true that we may yet become
what we might have been. That still remains his promise.
If only we would get back to Bethel; if only we would come
back to God.

And at Bethel, Jacob rediscovered the old prayer power.
Verses 1 and 13 tell us that God had talked with Jacob
there. Many times has God spoken clearly to this nation;
many times can we look back in our history and see that
God has spoken to America in his power, his presence, and
his deliverance. Many times has God spoken to us as individuals. You and I need to return to the place of real
prayer so that we may hear God speak again. How often
we think of prayer as nothing more than talking to God.
The need is to understand that God is seeking to say something to us. Perhaps you think you can't pray as before.
Maybe you think God doesn't hear you any more. Or you
may feel you don't have time to pray. But if you will go
back to that place where last you did business with God,
you will surely find God is still there; he is still ready. God
will hear your prayer.

Spurgeon tells of a little child who climbed to her father's
lap and said, "Poppa, is God dead?" And the daddy said,
"Well, why do you ask such a question, my child?" She
said, "Well, Daddy, I don't hear you talking to him any
more like you used to." Oh God, deliver America—God,
deliver American homes from daddies and mothers who do
not pray and who do not care. Deliver America from peo-

ple who are unconcerned. We need to "go back to Bethel" and rediscover protection, worship, honor, provision, and prayer. God is ready if we will come.

How does one find and travel the road to renewal? Look at verses 2-3. To be sure, there is a price to be paid for the journey. Some things need to be left behind; there is an effort to be put forth. When God called him back to Bethel, Jacob commanded those with him, "Put away the strange gods that are among you and be clean and change your garments and let us arise and go to Bethel."

Look at the three things he said. First, "put away your strange gods." Remember that little grave Jacob had dug out there under the oak tree at Shechem. It was there he buried Rachel's idols. He had tolerated those false gods, but the God of glory would have nothing to do with them; he told Jacob to bury them. For us, an idol is anything that takes the place of God in our life. For each idol in our lives, a burial service is needed. Our nation has worshiped, for instance, at the shrine of materialism long enough. If necessary, we need to bury our Cadillacs; bury our fine homes; bury our tailored lawns and carpeted living rooms. We need to put our idols away and turn to God. You will never go back, and you will never really listen to God if there is something standing between you and him or until you bury that thing that seems more important than the call of God in your life.

More than that, Jacob commanded his people to clean up. He referred to washing on the outside, but his real meaning was a cleansing of the heart. There is only one way for you to go back to God and that is to be clean. The only way to be clean is to be washed in the blood of the Lamb.

Finally, he said this: "Change your garments. The polluted ones will no longer do." There must be a willingness to come before God in modesty and meaning. Our nation needs to change to God's garments. I read in the newspaper where two hundred people were walking around nude on a public beach in California. They defended it, saying there is nothing wrong with nudity. Those who believe that, should listen to the Bible. The first animal sacrificed in the Bible was slain by God to cover the nudity of Adam and Eve. Nudity is a shame. Immodesty is a curse. We need to throw away the robes of our polluted sin and be robed in the righteousness of Jesus our Lord. If we would go back to God, we need to bow before him, confess our sin, and say as the song writer said:

> Lord Jesus, I long to be perfectly whole;
> I want Thee forever to live in my soul;
> Break down ev'ry idol, cast out ev'ry foe:
> Now wash me, and I shall be whiter than snow.

The Lord said to Jacob when he got back to Bethel, "I am El Shaddi, I am almighty God. Jacob you can reckon on me; you can count on me."

And God says to America today, "You've been counting on missles, bombers, and troops; I'll tell you that you can count on me and me alone." God admonishes you as an individual today that, if you've been counting on religious experience alone, you've been counting on something counterfeit. Let me tell you what to do. You come to Calvary. You bow at Bethel. You count on God, you trust Jesus his son, and he'll save you today. And God help you as you do.

Matthew 11:28-30

Come unto me, all ye that labour and are heavy laden, and I will give you rest.

Take my yoke upon you, and learn of me: for I am meek and lowly of heart: and ye shall find rest unto your souls.

For my yoke is easy and my burden is light.

4

Declaration of Dependence

On July 4, 1776, in the Continental Congress, representatives of the thirteen American colonies gave full and
formal approval of a resolution announcing the separation
of those colonies from Great Britain and thereby forming
an organization which became the United States of America.
That document was and is now known as the Declaration
of Independence.

The purpose of that hallowed declaration was to state the
clear-cut conviction of some brave men that they should
never again be oppressed by political powers from without.
No other document in the annals of history has been more
earnestly written, or made to describe more beautifully, the
freedom given to all men who desire it.

Each time I turn to that time-honored document, I become increasingly aware that it is something more than just
a declaration of independence. My conviction grows that
it could well be named a "Declaration of *Dependence.*" As
you read the first paragraph of the Declaration of Independence, you find that the men who wrote it started with God.
They stated that the liberties and rights they described are
given to man by nature and nature's God. You will find
them saying that all men are created equal and that they

are endowed by their Creator with certain inalienable rights. Read all of the Declaration; you will note especially that it concludes with this significant statement: "And for the support of this declaration, with a firm reliance on the protection of Divine Providence, we mutually pledge to each other our lives, our fortunes, and our sacred honor."

Out of that event our nation was born—a nation which has been racked with problems. A nation which has sometimes been guilty of errors. A nation which has been often maligned by its own self-appointed experts. Ours is a nation that through two hundred years of history has held out its arms to people all over the world with a gracious invitation for men to come and claim the victories that are made possible by America's first declaration of man's independence from political oppression and dependence upon God.

On the Statue of Liberty in New York harbor, these words come ringing clear:

> Not like the brazen giant of Greek fame with
>   conquering limbs astride from land to land,
> Here at our sea-washed sunset gates shall stand
>   a mighty woman with a torch whose flame is the
> Imprisoned lightning and her name "Mother of Exiles."
> From her beacon hand glows worldwide welcome;
> Her mild eyes command the air-bridged harbor that
>   twin cities form.
> "Keep ancient lands, your storied pomp!" cries she
>   with silent lips.
> "Give me your tired, your poor, your huddled masses
>   yearning to breathe free,
> The wretched refuse of your teeming shore,
> Send these, the homeless, tempest-tossed to me:
> I lift my lamp beside the golden door!"

Because of her outstretched arms of liberty in a glorious
invitation to all, America has become a haven to the homeless, food to the hungry, and opportunity to the oppressed.
She has truly been led of God to be "the land of the free
and the home of the brave." Yet today America is gripped
by the "paralysis of analysis." Men everywhere are be-
littling her. She has been criticized and picked apart from
many sources. In spite of the fact that she has walked
through two hundred years with all types of problems and
difficulties, no nation of people upon the face of the earth
has ever been more willing to tackle their problems and
work toward meaningful solutions. In spite of the fact that
there are racial tensions, social ills, and domestic and
foreign difficulties, these United States of America still form
the greatest land that has ever existed in the history of mankind.

I get tired of reading what is wrong with America. I
know there are problems. I know some things are wrong.
However, I am ready now to hear somebody again proclaim
what is *right* with America. There is much that is right
with this great land or she would not have stood this long.
Down through our history, hungry nations have come to
our shores to find food. Those unable to come have received supplies shipped from America's full coffers. During
our country's history, men have immigrated from all the
nations of the earth. You will find aliens, refugees, and
naturalized citizens in every part of our land. For each one
who comes, there are thousands of others yearning to reach
this land; eager to know something of the victory we hold
for the freedom of mankind.

America recognizes that freedom results from responsible citizenship and religious dependence. Inspired men

have made this country great. What we need today in our
lives as individuals and as a nation, is not a renewal of the
Declaration of Independence, but a new understanding of
our declaration of dependence upon God. We need to recognize that God is our strength and our refuge and our very
present help in time of trouble.

In our text, Jesus Christ stood calling men to a definite
dependence upon himself. Not as a cold marble statue
who lifts her lamp beside the door of a liberated nation.
Not as a dead hero of history who left behind some liber-
ating principles, but as the living Lord of heaven and earth,
Jesus Christ calls men unto himself. He calls men to depend
on him, to rest in him.

Ours is indeed a restless world. Never has this been more
evident than it is now. The cry goes up from millions on
the earth, "Oh, where may rest be found?" It is the desperate longing of the human heart to find a place of peace,
a haven of rest. Jesus stood one day amidst men in their
need—toiling, laboring, burdened, and restless humanity—
and issued his most gracious invitation to all mankind. His
words are a benediction to those on humanity's highway
who experience the depths of human need. Never have
more sublime words been uttered. Never has a more loving
invitation been extended than these words of Jesus Christ,
words of invitation for men to assume a yoke of dependence
which shall set them free.

We seek greater understanding from our text about our
Lord and what he wants to do in our lives as we live for
him day by day. I call your attention first of all in the text
to the universal proposal that Jesus has made. In the Scripture, Jesus says to men: "Come unto me, all ye that labour
and are heavy laden, and I will give you rest." Notice the

words are given in a meaningful offer. See who makes the offer. Words are meaningful only when the sovereign right of the one who speaks them is without question. In verse 27, you will find Jesus stating the central theme of the Christian faith: "All things are delivered unto me of my Father: and no man knoweth the Son, but the Father; neither knoweth any man the Father, save the Son, and he to whomsoever the Son will reveal him." That is Christ's statement regarding his authority. Here is the claim that he alone can reveal God unto man.

John 1:18 says that Jesus came from the bosom of the Father. Again in John 14:9 he declared for himself that he and the Father were one. "He that hath seen me, hath seen the Father." Such a claim from any other of the world's greats would be out of place. It would be an insult. Could you imagine hearing Aristotle, Socrates, Bacon, or any of the other great intellects saying: "I and God are one. I am the Son, he is the Father. We are one and no man knows the Father save in me?" It would be an affront had it come from the lips of any other man in the pages of history except the very lips of our Lord Jesus Christ—the one who walked the shores of Galilee and preached in the streets of Nazareth and Jerusalem the victorious message of salvation as God gives it in his grace. I call your attention to the fact that this is the One who makes the proposal. He is the one who says "Come unto me." He is the Son of God. He is the Savior of men.

Notice further, the one thing that he offers—himself. Jesus says: "Come unto me and to me alone. I will reveal unto you the nature of God and your need." This offer will not be found anywhere else. When Jesus invites men to rest in him, he invites them in a personal invitation to a personal relationship with himself. Jesus has not said: "Come to join my organization. Come join this particular political movement." Jesus says: "Come unto me and I myself, I the Son of God, will give you rest."

Next, take note to whom Christ makes the offer: *all!* He sets no limits around that blessed "all.'. Not to the favored few, but to all about him who were laboring for a living but longing for life. He saw men who were ostensibly seeking truth and meaning when they were actually seeking God. Jesus made God available unto these men. They were a burdened and oppressed people, and he called to them to find freedom and dependence on him. I believe Jesus Christ looked forward from that point in time, to see you and me in this hour and all men from that day until now. Jesus says to all men: "Come, depend upon me. Come rest in me. Come trust in me and in the Father with whom I am one. You shall find the rest you seek." He extends that universal proposal to all men. Jesus' call is externally contemporary. Jesus says to you—to me—to all men everywhere—"Come unto me and I will give you rest."

Not only is this a universal proposal, but it is a very unusual provision he makes. Jesus Christ says, "Take my yoke upon you and learn of me." Some would expect Jesus to say: "If you would rest, if you are weary, come with me, lie down and go to sleep." You would expect him to say: "Come and just take it easy. Come and you will find rest by doing nothing." Jesus Christ recognized the need of the human heart. He knows the nature of man, for he created him, and he does not call men to lie down on a bed of drowsy "do-nothingness." Jesus Christ has called men to a yoke of service and a school of conviction. The call of Christ is a call to commitment. Jesus said, "Come unto me, take a yoke upon you."

Jesus recognized, as all men ought, that there is no freedom without responsibility. This great United States of America, if she has made a mistake, has been in greatest error when she said to the thousands who are being borne to her shores every year, "Now you are an American, you do not have to do anything but sit around and complain because you do not get exactly what you want." We have made a mistake because we have not said to our people as a nation: "Give me your tired, your poor and your huddled masses that yearn to breathe free and I will give them a chance to be men. I will give them a chance to stand on their feet. I will give them a chance to have responsibility. I will give them an opportunity to extend themselves and to meet the challenge they have as human beings." That is what it is to be free.

Jesus Christ called men to a yoke of responsibility. Jesus was familiar with the yoke. William Barclay in his commentary said that maybe Jesus in his carpenter shop in Nazareth made the best yokes in all of the area. Perhaps Jesus might have had a sign over his carpenter shop that said, "My yokes fit well." We don't know if that is true, but at any rate Jesus was familiar with the yoke. Jesus offered to men to remove the yoke of the heavy burden and to give a yoke of grace. *The Interpreter's Bible* says: "For the burden of the law, . . . he offered his law of worship and love . . . For the yoke of selfish pride . . . Jesus offered his meek obedience and his lowliness of heart. For the load of "unchartered freedom," . . . Jesus offered his freedom—the freedom of dutiful sons of God the Father. For the burden of sin Jesus offered the joy of sins forgiven and the power of "an endless life." Jesus Christ called men unto commitment.

Jesus Christ also called men to freedom to dependence upon him in a provision of discipline. The next phrase says, "Learn of me." The word *learn* is the New Testament word for disciple. To be a disciple means to be a learner, to be a "follower after." The Master is saying: "You come, take your yoke, enroll in my school of instruction and come in commitment to be what I would have you be; pattern your life after my life.

We live in a day when the human heart rebels against discipline of any kind. In our time many clamor for abolition of all laws, standards of morality, rules, and restraints. We abolish capital punishment and decide that it is proper to have no deterrents whatsoever. We have repealed laws, removed restraints, lowered standards, and ridiculed moral codes—all in the name of human decency and justice. We have become a "do-your-own-thing" people. This has opened the door to indulgent permissiveness, resulting in all sorts of idiotic behavior. We vote ourselves all kinds of improved benefits with no thought of who is going to pay the bills. We have inflation because every man goes around with his hand outstretched.

Because of our many indiscretions, we need now to learn from those great men who founded this country. They said: "I declare my independence before men and my dependence upon God. I pledge my life, my fortune, and my sacred honor to that declaration." Instead, our theme song today seems to be: "Don't fence me in, I want to do my own thing. Don't bother me with your problems. Don't bother me with your difficulties. Just pad my check some more. Cross my palm with more money, and let me have more pleasures." Our nation is in trouble because she has evaded responsibility. We have refused to make commitments. We have found discipline distasteful. We need to learn again that those men who gave us what we have, were men of discipline.

On one occasion, I listened patiently to a very learned man as he argued articulately for some of today's indulgences. He reasoned with beautiful phrases about the hurt of humanity and how the government ought to take care of everybody. "Just dole it out," he said, "take care of everybody someway." I looked at that man and said: "Sir, all I know is that, if the men who formed this nation had agreed with the attitude you are talking about, you and I wouldn't be here right now. We would be somewhere grubbing out a meager living in a rice paddy.

Somebody cared, somebody paid, and armies made the supreme sacrifice to purchase our freedom. Our freedom comes from discipline and commitment. Jesus Christ said that the same principles apply spiritually. No man is made spiritually free until he commits himself to a disciplined life. Jesus Christ took two symbols that were repulsive to the people of his day—a yoke and a cross. Jesus said, "Wear my yoke, bear your cross, and follow after me."

Through the years some have forfeited eternal citizenship in heaven because they did not want to bear a yoke or a cross. They did not understand the spirit of the man who says, "Make me captive, Lord, and then I shall be free." Jesus insists that men give up their swords so they may conquer in love. It is a most unusual provision, but Jesus said that if you want to rest, you are not to come and lie down but come and put your strength in his yoke.

The spirit of dependence also issues forth from an undeniable paradox. Jesus went on to say, "My yoke is easy and my burden is light." How can a yoke be easy? How can a burden of discipline and responsibility be light? Some would suggest that the Christian life is anything but easy, and that is true. Life on earth was difficult for Jesus. He warned his disciples to be prepared to pay a high price for following him. Yet in this particular text Jesus' words mean, "My yoke is easy, kindly, it is well fitting and my burden is light." That means it is easy to bear. Nothing good just happens. If we are to be good citizens, we must also accept responsibilities. We can do this as long as we have a purpose which is worthy. Such is the case for those who follow Christ. The commands of Christ are great. We are confronted with challenge. How can we possibly find the yoke easy and the burden light? Let me share with you some ways we can do it.

First of all, the yoke is easy and the burden is light when we consider the alternatives. Let me illustrate by talking about our country again. If you don't like America, consider the alternatives. A well-known professional basketball player says this is not his country. Let that same basketball player go to some other country and try to make two million dollars bouncing a ball up and down a court. He doesn't like this country? Has he considered the alternative? Shake your fist at the flag. Shake your fist at this nation. Start crying and stop trying. Just consider the alternatives and see if you can find anything better. All over this world men are crying—yes, dying—to get to these shores. Why should we put up with a group of radicals who shake their fists and disclaim citizenship in this country? Consider the alternatives.

The same thing is true about Jesus. Some men say, "I don't want to be a Christian; it's too difficult. I won't be a

Christian because there are things I don't want to give up.
I don't want to be a Christian because that yoke is too
tough." Consider the alternative. Accept him, you get a
yoke and a cross. Accept him, you have responsibility
and discipline. Accept him and you walk with him in committed service. Accept him and you will reign with him in
glory. Your alternative—reject him and you have a burden
of sin. Reject him and you have unforgiven guilt in your
heart. Reject him and you are condemned to an eternity
in a devil's hell. You think Jesus' yoke is too much? Consider the alternative.

Something else of importance comes to us from our text.
Consider who shares your burden. Do you know how a yoke
is made? It is a wooden bar with two loops extending down-
ward from it. Do you know why it has two loops? It is so
two oxen can pull together in it. Jesus said, "It is my yoke
and so your part is to pull only one side." A yoke is not
made to make a burden heavy. A yoke makes it possible to
lift a burden. Jesus said, "Put your shoulder in the harness,
put your head in the yoke, and I'll take the other side and
together we shall conquer."

Stop to consider who is pulling the other side of the harness. No yoke can be too much when you are yoked with
the Lord of heaven and you pull together with him. The
only problem is in knowing how that yoke will ever touch
your shoulders—he will be pulling so far ahead of you. You
think his burden is too much? Consider how easy he makes
it. Matthew Henry said the most beautiful thing about this
text. He suggested Jesus' yoke is easy because he lines it
with love. Any burden given in love and carried in love is
always light. Augustine said that all things are light to love.

You remember that story in the Old Testament about

Jacob and Rachel? The Bible says that Jacob saw Rachel and he loved her. He made an agreement with her father that he would work for seven years so that he could have her to be his bride. Jacob was pretty deceptive, but he met a man who could match him in wit. Jacob worked seven years. Instead of receiving his beloved Rachel on his wedding night, his father-in-law secretly sent to the nuptial tent her older sister, Leah. When Jacob discovered that he was deceived, he went to the father who said, "It is only right that the older sister would marry first, but I'll tell you what to do. Work for me seven more years and the girl you love is yours today." And so Jacob labored seven years for Rachel (fourteen years altogether), and they seemed to him only a few days for the love he had for her.

"Come unto me, all ye that labour and are heavy laden and I will give you rest." Take my yoke upon you, Jesus is saying. Commit yourself in discipleship unto me. My yoke is easy, it is lined with love. A universal proposal, an unusual proposition, an undeniable paradox and unconditional promise.

We see a restless world all about us. Our restlessness leads us to feverish activity as we rush here and there trying to find rest. Jesus Christ, the Lord of heaven and earth, says, "Come unto me and I will give you rest." A great nation was born when brave men, bolstered by faith in God, declared their independence from England and their dependence upon heaven. Today that nation calls to the tired, the poor, the huddled masses yearning to breathe free, the wretched refuse of the world's teeming shores. Say anything you want to say about it, she is my country, the land that I love. There are many things right about America. As much as I love my country, I listen to a more urgent voice and I hear the Lord Christ. He calls men in love to wear the yoke of freedom. We are invited to come to him in salvation, to follow him in discipleship, to learn from him in fellowship, and to yoke up with him in partnership. Jesus Christ says, "Come unto me and I will give you rest."

Declare your independence from the devil today and declare your dependence upon God!

Hebrews 12:27 to 13:8

And this word, Yet once more, signifieth the removing of those things that are shaken, as of things that are made, that those things which cannot be shaken may remain.

Wherefore we receiving a kingdom which cannot be moved, let us have grace, whereby we may serve God acceptably with reverence and godly fear:

For our God is a consuming fire.

Let brotherly love continue.

Be not forgetful to entertain strangers: for thereby some have entertained angels unawares.

Remember them that are in bonds, as bound with them; and them which suffer adversity, as being yourselves also in the body.

Marriage is honourable in all, and the bed undefiled: but whoremongers and adulterers God will judge.

Let your conversation be without covetousness; and be content with such things as ye have: for he hath said, I will never leave thee, nor forsake theee.

So that we may boldly say, The Lord is my helper, and I will not fear what man shall do unto me.

Remember them which have the rule over you, who have spoken unto you the word of God: whose faith follow, considering the end of their conversation.

Jesus Christ the same yesterday, and to day, and for ever.

5

America's Unshakable Assurance

Our nation is "all shook up." Everywhere we look, the foundations of things we held unbreakable are reeling under the onslaught of queer quakings. The tremors that try men's souls are being felt on every frontier.

Trained on the tradition of revering our rulers as hallowed heroes, we Americans have borne the bitter disappointment of seeing some men misuse the sacred trust of public office to obtain personal possessions. Our confidence has been shaken.

Certain that our cause was just, we have commanded the respect of friend and foe and marched forward to the fray to win wars that were clearly right. Yet, because our personal integrity and national morality have sunk to substandard by any estimate, we have lost our fearless feeling of being just and are no longer able to purchase respect nor win wars. Our security is shaken.

Each day we are confronted by the fact that our constitutional rights are being taken away by bureaucratic bullies, who pass rulings at their pleasure. Perhaps this is caused by the fact that we have forgotten phrases from our most hallowed documents, such as the Declaration of Independence: "And for the support of this declaration, with a firm reliance on the protection of Divine Providence, we mutually pledge to each other our lives, our fortunes, and our sacred honor." Surely we have not pondered our pledge "one nation under God" as we ought. The United States was not founded by men fighting for fortune but by souls seeking God. The unshakable faith of our forefathers has been eroded and our souls are shaken.

In such a tremoring time, where is there a center of permanence? We need not an anchorage. An anchorage suggests hindrance, that which restricts and retards motion and progress. We need some element that is sure, unshakable. It has been proved by the most enlightened age of all time that such is not to be found in man's strength. As great as has been our country, so great can it be again if Americans can find an unshakable assurance.

Our text from Hebrews presents this center of permanence in the person of a King and a kingdom which cannot be shaken. Verse 26 of chapter 12 is part of a judgment statement. The writer declares throughout the book that God has spoken his final word through his Son. There is no escape for those who turn away, for a day is coming when he shall speak again from heaven. That speaking will be a message of judgment and not salvation. In such a day, he will shake (agitate, cause to tremble) once for all the earth and heaven at the second coming of Jesus Christ for final judgment.

When that final thrashing has been done and the harvest of God's wrath reaped, there will remain the kingdom of God which cannot be shaken. Moving to verse 28, we have our assurance and admonition. We, as believers in Jesus have already become citizens of that government which cannot be moved. This is our ground for calm trust in God and loyalty to Christ.

Here is our unshakable assurance. While we live on this earth, we are to be assured of strength. It comes not from man's maneuvering, but by God's grace. Looking to the final chapter of the Hebrew letter, we can see some statements which strengthen this assurance.

We find first, an unfailing promise. In 13:1-7, admonitions are given about practical expressions. Men are to live with concern for others. The home is to be hallowed. Allegiance is to be given to those in authority. Contentment with what we have is to comfort our hearts. How can these things be accomplished? In the last of verse 5 the power for such performance is presented: "For he hath said, I will never leave thee, nor forsake thee." With this promise, we need never fear what man may do, as verse 6 teaches. In the promise are five negatives strengthening each other. The literal statement of the phrase might well be written, "I will never, never leave thee nor never, never, never forsake thee."

The promise of God's word can never be shaken. All the documents of declaration may decay, but his word is for always. Jesus said, "Heaven and earth shall pass away, but my words shall not pass away" (Mark 13:31).

"He hath said." What power prevails in that promise. The person who can by faith lay claim to this has an all-conquering weapon with which doubt is dismissed. All that God is and all he has, he has given to his people in this promise. The strength of the assurance is in the simple acceptance of God's Word to man's need.

There are at least five occasions in Scripture wherein God has promised never to leave nor forsake his own. As we examine these, our assurance is strengthened even further.

In Genesis 28:15 we find this promise posed to a man in trials. Jacob was a man whose life seemed beset by trial. In the passage from Genesis, he is seen fleeing from his father's house because of his brother's wrath. Under the sparkle of the stars he sleeps in the loneliness of night. There God makes the promise, "I will never, never leave thee."

See the steps Jacob takes along the way from that point of promise. Watch in the Word as he is cheated by Laban, but God never leaves him. He flees with Laban hard on his heels, but in Mizpah's Mount God makes his foe his friend. Later on, the pursuit of his offended brother Esau turns to a joyous reunion. In his old age, Jacob goes down to Egypt to see his son, Joseph. Through it all, Jacob declares it so, "God will never forsake his own."

For us today, individually and nationally, whatever may be the sore trials of our situation, the promise is to him who believes: "I will never leave thee; I will never forsake thee."

Next we find the promise given to a people facing challenge. In Deuteronomy 31:6 it is so stated. Here we see Israel preparing to advance into Canaan. They were to fight the accursed nations and drive out the giants who had chariots of iron. They stood in the strength of his promise, and he did not forsake them until from Dan to Beersheba the chosen seed possessed the promised land.

Such a challenge faces the church of God in our shaking times. God's people are called to turn this nation again to spiritual strength. We would shudder at the assignment and shrink from its challenge were it not for the promise that we may move on from one conquest to another in the power of his presence. To know that her Lord can never leave his church should cause her to attempt more for his glory. So likewise should a nation of men bow before his

presence and then stand in his name to renew her character
and strengthen her stand for liberty.

Again, in Joshua 1:5, the promise is given to a leader looking for courage. The young man, Joshua, had been called to
stand in the shoes of the mystic Moses, and to him God
made the promise, "I will never leave thee, nor forsake thee."
In that assurance, Joshua led the people on to victory. In
our nation today, as well as in our churches, there is a need
for leaders who will bear the heat of the battle. The reason
many falter in fear is because we seek to stand in our own
strength rather than in the promise of God's power. To the
man called to courageous leadership, there comes upon his
commitment to God the unfailing promise, "I will never
forsake thee."

Again, the assurance is claimed in 1 Chronicles 28:20
when tasks are needing completion. In this passage David
is giving instructions to Solomon for the building of the
Temple. "Be strong and of good courage, and do it: fear
not, nor be dismayed: for the Lord my God, will be with
thee; he will not fail thee, nor forsake thee, until thou hast
finished all the work."

Here is much to be learned. If only American leaders
would return to the basics of building a nation of liberty
and freedom such as our fathers started, we would find
our greatest hope. These fathers have handed us a heritage
as did David to Solomon. When the Queen of Sheba suggested false foreign policies, God did not leave Solomon,
and God's wisdom delivered Solomon. When domestic
difficulties caused two starving harlots to seek a decision,
Solomon found the wisdom of his never failing God sufficient. The Temple was built, one stone upon another
until completion came.

There is all that America needs to face her foes and feed her friends. It is in the promise of God. As we look to him, he will give us guidance for foreign affairs, decency in domestic difficulties, and victory in our relationship to all peoples.

Again we see the assertion in Isaiah 41:17. "When the poor and needy seek water, and there is none, and their tongue faileth for thirst, I the Lord will hear them, I the God of Israel will not forsake them."

America's unshakable assurance can come unhindered in the power of the promise that all who seek salvation in Christ may come and drink deeply from the waters of life's wells. Our country has sought after many things to find only that the things she trusted in have become less than certain. Individuals have vainly searched in ceremonies and religious rituals for peace in heart. It may seem to some that we as a people have gone too far for even God to help us. But the promise to a repentant people is, "I will not forsake them."

Thank God that in a shaking world our chart and compass are secure! The Book is reliable. The promises of God are unfailing. He will never, never leave, nor never, never, never forsake his own.

> The soul that on Jesus hath leaned for repose
> I will not, I will not desert to his foes.
> That soul, though all hell should endeavor to shake,
> I'll never, no never, no never forsake!

Our unshakable assurance lies in knowledge of an unchanging person. One of the greatest trials of our time has been in the failure of folks in whom we had placed our assurance. Graft and corruption are common. Some who once were solid have changed and now seem sordid. Where can we put our trust?

The writer to the Hebrews tells us in 13:8 ff. the answer to the perplexity. We do not need to be worried and carried about by every wind and perplexed by many persons. There is one who changes not. Ours is not the need of a new prophet or a latter-day savior. Political heroes will not accomplish what our country desperately needs. The need of America and Americans is to place our faith in him who is unshakable, the unchanging Lord Jesus Christ.

He is the unchanging Redeemer of yesterday. To think of the yesterday of our Lord overwhelms us with infinity. He is eternal, therefore, without beginning. The yesterday must include his preexistence, his creative work, his place in the triune councils of heaven; however, for our present understanding we turn to the yesterday of what the New Testament calls "the days of his flesh." Here we see Jesus becoming man, bearing man's sorrow, and dying for man's sin. He, the unchanging Redeemer of yesterday, is the same today. He has, through his flesh, purchased pardon for all who come unto him by faith.

The same Jesus is the unchanging Intercessor of today. Constantly the author of the text refers to Christ as our great high priest who sits at the throne of God to make intercession for us. In the last days of his flesh, he told his disciples that they should see him no more in a little while, but soon they should see him without the limitation of the flesh. It is so today. Jesus may be known intimately as he lives within by the Spirit. While other helpers fail and comforts cease, he is the unchanging priest and the all-sufficient Savior for those who live by faith.

This same Jesus is the unchanging Victor of tomorrow.

With God there is no time; however, as men we must so think. There is a tomorrow with God. A tomorrow where the ultimate battle shall be done, the victory won. In this tomorrow, Christ shall be the unchanging center of victory. He shall never grow weary. Heaven will never become monotonous. There will always be in the unchanging Christ an unshakable satisfaction for the heart.

Yes, America's assurance lies in an unchanging Champion, not a political promiser who offers, at best, only man's unsure options; her hope is in him who is the same yesterday, today, and forever.

> Abide with me: fast falls the eventide;
> The darkness deepens; Lord, with me abide:
> When other helpers fail, and comforts flee,
> Help of the helpless, O abide with me!
>
> Swift to its close ebbs out life's little day;
> Earth's joys grow dim, its glories pass away;
> Change and decay in all around I see:
> O Thou who changest not, abide with me!

Our text not only presents an unfailing promise and an unchanging person in which and upon whom we can believe, but it reveals to us an unmistakable purpose for our lives and for our nation. We see this presented in Hebrews 13:20-21.

In looking to our shaking world, many question the purpose, the end to which it all points. Perhaps the reason for so much discontent and dismay has been that we have become a people without purpose. Rather than pioneers preaching freedom and sacrificing for its attainment, ours has become a nation of luxury and laxity. The ultimate purpose for a people that should be unshakable is in the work and purpose of God.

The Hebrew nation had undergone trials which no doubt created questions about the new revelation in Christ. Added to this was the conflict within the church over the authority of her leaders. The author now speaks to them a benediction which assures that the purpose of God is to bring them peace, and he has the power to perform that purpose. Here is the only direct allusion to the resurrection of Jesus in the entire epistle. This is the seal of God upon all that is done.

God's purpose is to bring together the broken or scattered. "To perfect" them so that all the members may be equipped with all the necessary means to enable them to do God's will. They were to make a definite break with Jewish traditions and nationalism and stand in the kingdom of Christ.

In our unstable, shaking world, where many seem to search for a purpose, the gospel of the kingdom offers that purpose. It is God working in his own that which is well pleasing in his sight. The unalterable purpose of our Lord is to draw us to himself and to live out in us his saving life. When we have surrendered to this purpose, we are the children of the Father who cannot be shaken.

In conclusion, let us state again, America will find her assurance when she finds her righteousness in Christ and relates herself to being "the people of God" that she once was. Americans, and all others, may find a certain anchor, an unshakable assurance in God's unfailing promise, through his unchanging Son, to work his unmistakable purpose. Let every Christian rejoice that in a shaking world there are some things which cannot be moved.

Galatians 2:15-21

We who are Jews by nature and not sinners of the Gentiles,

Knowing that a man is not justified by the works of the law, but by the faith of Jesus Christ, even we have believed in Jesus Christ, that we might be justified by the faith of Christ, and not by the works of the law: for by the works of the law shall no flesh be justified.

But if, while we seek to be justified by Christ, we ourselves also are found sinners, is therefore Christ the minister of sin? God forbid.

For if I build again the things which I destroyed, I make myself a transgressor.

For I though the law am dead to the law, that I might live unto God.

I am crucified with Christ: nevertheless I live; yet not I, but Christ liveth in me: and the life which I now live in the flesh I live by the faith of the Son of God who loved me, and gave himself for me.

I do not frustrate the grace of God: for if righteousness come by the law, then Christ is dead in vain.

Did These Die in Vain?

Memorial Day is a uniquely American experience. The Memorial Day observance was begun during the Civil War when some concerned and thoughtful ladies decided to decorate the graves of men who had bravely given their lives in that destructive civil conflict between the states.

The day is intended to stir us to grateful recall of all those who have given themselves, who have shed their blood, who have laid down their lives in military battle for the cause of freedom in our land.

Our freedoms have not been easily won. The price of freedom is always great. For men to determine their own destiny, they have always been confronted by the risk of conflict against those who would seek to rule over them. Such has been the pattern in these United States.

Nearly five centuries ago, European explorers discovered the North American continent, a vast, fruitful expanse created by a loving God. The thrilling discovery of a new world opened the door for a steady stream of other Europeans convinced they could find their destinies here.

When around the turn of the seventeenth century they began to settle in places such as Jamestown and Plymouth, they discovered anew that the struggle for freedom is always

77

great. Despite the absence of a major war, the first seven months at Jamestown saw the population reduced from 105 to 32 people, partly because of the opposition of Indians but primarily because of starvation and exposure. Their new land was potentially a land of plenty, but it was not, at that time, so plentious. Those men and women, braving the storms of that first wintertime, died by the numbers. They literally gave themselves in order to cut a small niche in a wilderness. Little by little, the continued efforts of our hardy forebears transformed that wilderness into the land of the free, the home of the brave, and the provision of plenty for the hungry multitudes that have teemed to her shores since that day. The price of freedom was exacted from our forefathers from the very beginning, and they died for the freedom they had sought.

We ask ourselves today, "Did those people die in vain? Was it for no avail?" Down through two hundred years there have been those who would say that they did not die in vain because this land has given so much to so many. In our day, however, the present generation appears almost ready to declare that perhaps those people did die in vain. Today's scoffers reason, our forefathers died, at least in part, believing the new world was the key to providing food for the world's hungry. That their faith was accurate is seen in America's vast capacity for food production. But we must admit their dream is only partially fulfilled in view of the alarming fact that two billion of the world's three billion go to bed hungry each night. Thus, some are saying today that our forefathers' sacrifice was in vain.

After years of struggle by the early colonists in forging our valued freedoms, the threat continued that imperialistic powers would drain away the productivity of the people of this nation.

Increasingly, citizens of the colonies stood against such oppression so that by 1775 they began to speak out boldly. Men like Patrick Henry, Thomas Paine, and others became spokesmen for the cause of freedom. Their sentiments seemed to be summarized by Patrick Henry's famous speech, "The War Inevitable," given during March of that year. His impassioned plea remains one of the most famous utterances of American History. He said: "Is life so dear and peace so sweet so as to be purchased at the price of chains and slavery? Forbid it almighty God. I know not what course others may take but as for me, give me liberty or give me death."

Representatives to the Continental Congress met a few months later in the city of Philadelphia to declare their independence and to disassociate themselves from those who would seek to drain away America's valuable resources. War inevitably came from that historic declaration. Farmers took down their squirrel guns from fireplace hangers to become defenders of freedom. Outnumbered and poorly equipped, they went out with resolute bravery to defeat the greatest army the civilized world had known to that time. Brave men stood in defense of freedom. Their blood was shed and many of them died. But the world will long remember their heroic, victorious stand.

In this day, we ask ourselves the question: "Did those men die in vain?" Some modern critics would insist they did. These moderns themselves are perhaps the gravest source of doubt about the value of the early settlers' labors. People around us are smirking at our liberties. Some ingrates cast aspersion against our leaders. Others laugh in the face of the constitution and of constitutional government. When we see people mocking our fine tradition of patriotism, perhaps we would say of at least some in this generation that our founding fathers died for nothing.

When we hear young people say, "This is not my country . . ." or "I don't care about this country"; when we hear politicians berating the flag, the government, and the President, we may ask ourselves again, "Did these die in vain?"

In 1861 a disastrous war broke out between the states. For four years a great price was again paid for the cause of freedom. The issue that brought about that critical conflict was whether the freedoms of this nation were to be made available to all men, be they black or white. Conviction and concern prompted many men to die; good men on both sides of the conflict. As a result, there was established at least a philosophy that all men *are* created equal and do have equal rights.

At this bicentennial time, we ask ourselves if the casualties of the Civil Ward died in vain? If we cannot now offer the freedoms of this nation to all men regardless of race, color, and creed, then we must admit to prejudice and, therefore, agree that perhaps those brave men died for naught.

In 1917, while Germany was waging war all over Europe, we went about business as usual, secure in the notion that the United States, with her modern weapons, advanced communications, and rapid transportation was safely isolated from that war. Many people in that day felt the nation should remain isolationist but we learned that a caring nation cannot remain aloof when a war is being waged on mankind. American ships were attacked on the high seas by German submarines. American men began to fall victims of German onslaughts. The President of the United States, Woodrow Wilson, said, "This is an attack. This is warfare on mankind. We must enter the conflict. We must fight for the cause that the world might be made safe for democracy."

With that, the United States was plunged into the worldwide conflict. Men by the thousands left their homes and families and went to fight the war of that time.

In the streets and cities of our country, people marched with flags unfurled and patriotic songs bursting from their hearts. During one of the worst flu epidemics this country has ever known, citizens forgot themselves and their needs in order to support the cause of freedom.

After the victory was won and the conflict ended, a tally revealed that more than a hundred thousand men had died, half of them from battle wounds and half from disease on the battlefield. We pause to ask ourselves the question: "Did these men die in vain?"

I could believe that if you look at some people about you, you would insist that casualties of America's wars died in vain. For instead of seeing people in our day giving expression of loving devotion to God and country, you see the flag of the United States of America sewn on the seat of the pants of idle youth whose contributions to society and even to their own welfare is subject to serious question. One wonders how long America should tolerate those who live by her generosity but viciously tear away her vitality.

Our forefathers died in vain if we are going to permit that much disregard for the price they paid for the freedoms they bought for us.

December 7, 1941, Japan waged her infamous attack on Pearl Harbor. Men from the United States lay dying.

Equipment, arms, and ships were blasted to pieces. On December 8, 1941, with only one dissenting voice, Congress voted war. The United States of America was again plunged into a worldwide conflict. Once again we learned the futility of isolationism. There is no way to maintain that position when world conflict is taking place, when men are encroaching upon the freedom of others. We were drawn into another conflict and many men—some of them your sons, your husbands, your fathers, your grandfathers—died in World War II.

We could ask ourselves the question: "Did they die in vain?"

Look around and observe people who are mocking our government and our freedoms: people who are saying that it is all for nothing; that we ought not to be concerned about the affairs of men throughout this world; that war ought to never be. Though we abhor war, we must recognize that as long as Satan and sin are in the world and man's nature is basically selfish, there will be war in defense of freedom. Some say we ought to never enter into war, but they wouldn't have breath to breathe or food to eat had not somebody died in World War II thirty years ago. Did these die in vain?

Men were dying recently in Vietnam. Did they die for naught? Some people sat at home in a soft arm chair, watching television, sipping on a drink, and criticizing the President. They said that our men there in the Vietnamese jungle were dying for nothing. It's much easier to be an expert in an easy chair than it is to serve on the battlefield or occupy the President's chair.

We hear people saying that these men died in vain. But listen with me to a man named Jesse Goodwin who was once chairman of the deacons in this church. Jesse lived more than a year in Saigon as a civil employee of the United States Government. In a letter he wrote: "Pastor, I believe with all of my soul that God is using this horrible conflict for a two-fold purpose: First to call one nation to him— that nation being South Vietnam; and secondly, to call another nation back to him—that being the United States of America."

You arm chair experts who enjoy the protection of America's vast strength, your carpings are at odds with the spirit of the man who in Christian love serves every day, rolls up his sleeves, and says: "Pastor, if you can send a few clothes, or some food, or some money, our little church is trying to show the South Vietnamese people that somebody in the name of Jesus really cares."

John F. Kennedy, shot down and slain in the streets of these United States, did he die in vain? Think of the assassinations that have followed. Remember all the lawlessness that is still here. See if you do not agree that we have fostered a disrespect for law and for our leaders. If you listen to people who enjoy a menu of cooked President, fried governor, and boiled senator and thereby prompt their young people to grow up thinking disrespect for government is the norm, then you might say that John F. Kennedy was slain in the streets of Dallas and nobody learned anything from it.

It's up to you and me whether or not these brave men have died in vain. They entrusted us with freedoms. They entrusted us with the stewardship of plenty. They provided us with opportunity. They gave us the opportunity to be the greatest people on the earth. They bequeathed us a chance to share freedom with the last man upon the earth.

Communication and transporation are available in our day
so that, if we have the courage and the stamina for it, we
could see peace come to many multitudes who have never
had anything but war. The means are available if we are
unselfish enough to continue the course that others have
died to open for us.

We shall never do it until it's done in the name of another
who has died. He fought in no wars. He marched in no
armies. He simply walked the streets of Judea two thousand years ago. He made the blind see and lame people
walk. He healed broken hearts and bound up the wounded.
He was so despised and rejected that a cruel cross was laid
on his back. Under that load he struggled out of the city
of Jerusalem to a hill called Golgotha, the place of the
skull. There that man Jesus Christ, the blessed Son of God,
the heaven-sent messenger of love, extended himself upon
that cross. They drove spikes in his hands; they pushed
thorns in his brow; they spat in his face; they gave him vin-
egar to drink; they slapped him with reeds and the backs of
their hands; they laughed him to scorn, and they thrust a
spear in his side. There God's Son, the blessed one of
heaven, died to defeat sin. The question is: "Did Jesus
die in vain? What good has it done? What good will it do?
What does the death of Jesus mean?"

There are those in our day who say: "Yes, Jesus died in
vain because we are not saved by his death; we're saved by
his life, by his example. We are saved by all the good things
Jesus did." There is a Christianity of ideals, good works,
and philanthropy in our day that seeks to remove the blood
of Christ out of the Christian gospel. To do that is to make
God a murderer and Christ a fool who died for nothing on
Calvary's hill.

Did Jesus Christ die in vain? Perhaps the answer to that question is yes. Yes, Jesus Christ died in vain . . . if salvation comes by any other means. If there is any other way under the sun, if there is any other way conceived in the mind of men, if there is any other way that could ever bring salvation to the lives of the lost, then Jesus Christ died in vain. If salvation is achieved, as some think, by man's goodness, Jesus died in vain.

People frequently say, "I don't think that man is naturally a sinner. I don't think that man is naturally bad. Man is naturally good. A man is saved by being good." My reply always is that if the best man who ever lived on the earth, a man who had the best habits and the least bad habits and did the most good for other people, if that man was saved by his goodness, then God is a murderer and Christ died a fool's death. There was no use in it. If one man could be saved by being good, all men could be saved the same way and Jesus didn't need to die.

Jesus died in vain if salvation comes in the name of any other savior. I'm frequently asked by people: "What about the Muhammadans; what about the Buddhists? They believe in God. Don't you think they might be saved?" If I could be saved by believing in Muhammed, a religious man who lived, who died, and whose bones are still in his tomb, then everybody could be saved by believing in him and nobody would have needed Jesus. God was foolish for letting Jesus die. He died in vain.

In Acts we read that there is none other name given under heaven among men whereby you must be saved. That name is Jesus.

Jesus died in vain if salvation comes by the works of the law. That was Paul's message to the Galatians. He said, "If righteousness comes by the law, if I could be made righteous by keeping the law of Moses, then there never was any use in Jesus Christ dying and it was all in vain." What Paul is saying is simply this: If we can be saved by being good, if we do not need Christ to be saved, then we can go back to Judaism. We can go back to the Old Testament law. We can go beyond grace. We can live by the law. Righteousness could be achieved through the law, and that then is the way to be saved. Yes, Christ died in vain if salvation comes by any other means.

Christ died in vain if grace cannot produce righteousness. Some friends often say: "You believe that 'once-saved-always-saved' business. If I believed that, then I would believe that man could simply walk down a church aisle, trust Jesus as his Savior, and then go out and live like hell, yet still go to heaven." Let me tell you something. The man who makes that statement doesn't understand about the grace of God. He knows nothing about salvation by grace. A person cannot believe in salvation by grace and, at the same time, refuse to believe in eternal security of the believer.

If you believe that salvation is not eternal when Jesus gives it to us, then it must be true that you believe you must work to receive it and work to keep it. If you must work to keep salvation, then you must work to get it. Let me tell you emphatically that salvation is by the grace of God. The grace of God is sufficient to change the heart of a man, to make him want to serve God out of love and honor and not out of fear of going to hell.

If the only reason I had for serving God was fear of going to hell, I could close my Bible and just give hell its sway in my life right now. The amazing grace of God and the redeeming blood of Jesus Christ that save me are sufficient to call forth from me a response of loving service to God. If God's grace in Christ isn't sufficient to change a man's heart and make him a new creature, if his grace isn't as Paul said, sufficient to make a person crucified to self and alive to God in Christ, then we don't need it. If God's grace in Christ is powerless to make a man a new creature, then Jesus died a fool's death and there wasn't any sense in it.

Jesus died in vain as far as you are concerned if you don't receive him as your Savior. If Jesus Christ died to save men from their sin and if, in fact, men can be saved by faith in Jesus by inviting him into their hearts, and if, in fact, you don't for yourself personally repent of your sin and personally accept him as your Savior, then you are as lost and headed for hell as you can be. As far as you are concerned, Jesus died in vain. It is an individual matter and you must decide.

Did Christ die in vain? Yes, if these things are true, he certainly did. But you say: "Preacher, I don't believe it. There must be more." And you're right! I'll join you in a victorious shout: "No, No! He didn't die in vain!"

Let us see why he did not die in vain. First of all, because of the need of man. Man needs a Savior. We read in the Bible that man is a sinner and sin brings death. Man must suffer death, the inevitable penalty of sin. Man consequently needs help in a desperate way. Jesus Christ, the God-man, living as man without sin, owing no penalty for his own sin, went to the cross and died for us. I know Jesus didn't die in vain because he meets your need and mine. You are not naturally good. You are naturally evil. You are naturally sinful. You are naturally selfish. You are lost in your natural state. You need a Savior, and Jesus Christ died to be your Savior.

The symbol of the New Testament church is not a table of stone, a seven branch lamp stand, a halo about a submissive head, or a crown of triumph. The symbol of the Christian church is a heavy, cruel, rugged Roman cross. The symbol of the Christian church is a fount of redeeming blood. It is the substitutionary act of a Savior who died for men in their sin. Jesus didn't die in vain, because you need him, and I need him.

There is another reason why Jesus Christ didn't die in vain. It is the message of the Scripture. If there is one word of truth in the Book, then Jesus Christ died for the salvation of men's souls. Read it from the Old Testament to the New. The theme of this Book is the cross and the death of Jesus. The blood shed in the Garden of Eden to hide our naked parents in their sin was symbolic of Jesus Christ's death for our sin. The sacrifice of Abel was symbolic of the blood of Jesus Christ. The offering of Isaac on the mount by his father, Abraham, was symbolic of the sacrifice of Jesus. The Passover lamb in Egypt when the blood was sprinkled on the door posts for the deliverance of people from the death angel pointed to the coming of the Lamb of God to take away the sins of the world. The Levitical offerings and the sacrifices spoke of the death of Jesus. The message of the prophets was of the coming Messiah, Jesus Christ, the Suffering Servant of God who died for the sins of men.

The New Testament is the story of the death of Jesus. John the Baptist opened his ministry by saying, "Behold the Lamb, the sacrifice of God, who takes away the sins of the world." One-fourth of the content of the Gospels

deals with the last days and death of Jesus Christ. Jesus
himself spoke often of his death. He opened his ministry
on that theme in the second chapter of John. In John 3
he said that the Son of man must be lifted up on the cross
even as the serpent was lifted up in the wilderness that men
might have life. To the Greeks who came to see him in John
12, he spoke of his death. To Mary who anointed him, he
said, "It is against the day of my burial." At the Last Sup-
per he inaugurated a memorial to his death. The preaching
of the disciples was filled with the death of Jesus. The focal
point of the gospel of Christ is that he died for our sin and
arose to give us eternal life. Jesus did not die in vain, because we need a Savior. The Bible declares he died for that
salvation.

Finally, Jesus did not die in vain, because there is salvation for all who will accept it. You can be saved today.
Multitudes have been saved. Many are being saved in the
name of Jesus Christ. The greatest proof you could ever
want for the effectiveness of the death of Jesus is the vast
number of men whose lives have been changed and whose
souls have been saved for eternity. If you want proof, look
around you. You will see the power of Christ's gospel
demonstrated in the lives of those who have been redeemed.

Did the heroes of our country die in vain? The answer is
up to you and me. It depends on what we do with the heritage they have given us. Did the hero of the Gospels die
in vain? The answer lies in what you and I do with him. If
you lived a long life in this land of plenty, were born into
a good family, had never wanted for food, acquired an education, worked at a good job, amassed a fortune, retired at
the early age of fifty, played championship golf until you
were seventy—had a cold, got over it—lived till you were

eighty-five, died in your sleep, were buried in a gold coffin, and left a million dollar fortune to your heirs but did not know Jesus Christ as your personal Savior, *it all would be in vain.*

Did Jesus die in vain? It depends simply on whether *you* accept him as your personal Savior. Why don't you do it today?

Romans 13:1-14

Let every soul be subject unto the higher powers. For there is no power but of God: the powers that be are ordained of God.

Whosoever therefore resisteth the power, resisteth the ordinance of God: And they that resist shall receive to themselves damnation.

For rulers are not a terror to good works, but to the evil. Wilt thou not then be afraid of the power? do that which is good, and thou shalt have praise of the same:

For he is the minister of God to thee for good. But if thou do that which is evil, be afraid; for he beareth not the sword in vain: for he is the minister of God, a revenger to execute wrath upon him that doeth evil.

Wherefore ye must needs be subject, not only for wrath, but also for conscience sake.

And for this cause pay ye tribute also: for they are God's ministers, attending continually ypon this very thing.

Render therefore to all their dues: tribute to whom tribute is due; custom to whom custom; fear to whom fear, honour to whom honour.

Owe to no man any thing, but to love one another: for he that loveth another hath fulfilled the law.

For this, Thou shalt not commit adultery, Thou shalt not kill, Thou shalt not bear false witness, Thou shalt not covet; and if there be any other commandment, it is briefly comprehended in this saying, namely, Thou shalt love thy neighbour as thyself.

Love worketh no ill to his neighbour: therefore love is the fulfilling of the law.

And that, knowing the time, that now it is high time to awake out of sleep: for now is our salvation nearer than when we believed.

The night is far spent, the day is at hand: let us therefore cast off the works of darkness, and let us put on the armour of light.

Let us walk honestly, as in the day; not in rioting and drunkenness, not in chambering and wantonness, not in strife and envying.

But put ye on the Lord Jesus Christ, and make not provision for the flesh, to fulfil the lusts thereof.

7
The Christian Citizen

"Owe no man any thing but to love one another; for he that loveth another hath fulfilled the law" (Rom. 13:8).

Lawlessness, contempt for authority, rebellion, sin, and crime are upon us like a flood. Lawlessness is the essence of sin. The Bible teaches that the last days before the Savior's second coming will be marked by increasing lawlessness. In his great prophetic discourse in Matthew 24:12, our Lord Jesus Christ said that in the last days "iniquity [or lawlessness] shall abound."

Seeing uncontrolled sin about us every day should certainly strengthen our conviction that the rising tide of evil indicates, above everything else, that we are approaching the second coming of our Lord. Lawlessness does abound. Rebellion and sin come down upon us like the waters of a flood. Many people have lost respect for authority in any area of life. This very destructive attitude is spelled out for us in the New Testament Scriptures.

One scholar has suggested that there are at least four Greek words used in the New Testament that present the idea of lawlessness. One is the word *komos* which means "revelings." In Galatians 5:19-21, this same word is translated that way. Literally the word *komos* pictures a troup of intoxicated revelers who, at the close of an orgy, wearing garlands on their heads, carrying torches in their hands, wander through the streets, singing and shouting insults and wanton outrage upon everyone they meet. We need nothing more than to recall recent events to see that kind of iniquity in a more modern setting. The past fifteen years have produced repeated scenes of uncontrolled fury heaped by men upon their fellowmen. The alleged causes have been but little more than confused concoctions of twisted logic.

Another expression in the New Testament is *ecthra* which means "hatred" or "enmity." It is similar to jealousy between men and classes of men. It may apply to nations but it also may occur within a nation, often within the fellowship of a particular family and all too frequently it creeps into the life of the church.

Still another New Testament word for lawlessness is *asotia* meaning "abandon," or complete oblivion to all control. The force of the word is perfectly illustrated in the experience of the prodigal son in Luke 15:11-32. Luke says that the young man went away from home and wasted his substance in riotious living. Our word *abandon* gives a better translation than does the word *riotious*. He wasted his life in abandonment.

To understand the meaning a little better, we can borrow some terminology of men who play professional football. It has often been said that they play football with reckless abandon. It means they throw their bodies into the game without regard for possible injury or for the hurt of anyone else. To a football player, that's a distinct compliment but, to use the word as it applies in the prodigal son's experience, it means those people who live their lives with a complete abandon from restraint with no thought for the future and no concern for the control of God or government.

The fourth word is perhaps the best known. *Anomia,* as used in 1 John 3:4 and other places, means to have contempt for the law. From base contempt comes rejection of control. The word comes closest to the force described in Romans 13. It is exactly the same word that Jesus used in Matthew 24:12 when he said that in the last days lawlessness or iniquity shall abound.

We know, of course, that sin was in the world long before the law. The Bible gives clear reason for us to believe that at least twenty-five hundred years before the law, sin was in the world.

Many people have the idea that first of all God made laws, and then man broke the law and sinned. Such is not the case at all. Man first of all sinned and then God gave the law. The purpose of the law was good. The purpose of the law was to point man back to God, to bring man into fellowship with God.

God is a God of government. God is a being of law and of organization. We need only to look at the world around us. Observe, for instance, your finger and see it respond to the mental command of your brain. By divine creation, God makes it happen. By this we know that God is a God of organization. Therefore, we see that if we are to be right with God, we will not be a lawless people.

The lawlessness of the last days is upon us everywhere. In contempt for treaty obligations on the part of nations, we see it. In disregard for old-time honesty in private contracts, we experience it. In the breaking loose of flaming youth from parental restraint; in the rush to expressionism whether in school dramatics or in disdain for the "old fogey" morals; in the calling of sin, lasciviousness, and adultery by modern names such as sex experience; in the flood of murder magazines and mystery novels, movies, and hard-core pornography; in the unwillingness of the public to have crime really punished; in showing public sympathy with sin—we must admit that the lawlessness that Jesus said would be true of the last days is upon us like a tidal wave.

Now the question you and I face is how a Christian is to live in this time of abandonment to lust and license. What is to be our attitude toward the government and civil authority? The restlessness of today is really deep lawlessness and God has called it sin. Sin is lawlessness, and lawlessness is sin. In 2 Thessalonians the Antichrist is called the lawless one. We are taught that the only thing that restrains lawlessness at all is the fact that God has still left his Spirit in the world. When the Lord Jesus comes for his church, however, and calls his church out of the world and the work of the Spirit is ended, the restraints will be lifted and lawlessness shall reign upon this earth without any restraint during the time of the great tribulation. These are signs of the coming again of our Lord Jesus Christ. But right now, as lawlessness, rebellion, and sin abound until the coming of the Lord, we raise the question as to how Christians are to live, as citizens of both the Kingdom of God and the civil government.

I believe it is important that we come to understand what the Scripture has to say concerning our respect for government and its officials.

First, in verses 1-7 of our text, Paul gives instructions about Christian citizenship. The passage points out to Christians the manner of living as citizens of the world. It presents a picture of the Christian and his secular life. The first thing Paul says is that we must recognize God as the power behind every higher power there is. He tells us in verse 1: "For there is no power but of God; the powers that be are ordained of God" and he says again in verse 4: "For he is the minister of God to thee for good."

We need, therefore, to understand that God inaugurated government. Look backward to Genesis 9:6 and you will find that when Noah had safely endured the flood, God said to Noah: "If by man's hand, man's blood is shed, so that same man's blood shall be shed by other men." In that straightforward declaration, God put the sword of the magistrate in the hand of Noah and established the principle of capital punishment for the crime of murder. It appears we live in a time when society is so sophisticated we feel we're smarter than God and we have outlawed capital punishment. We have decided that we are too humane to punish criminals. But God, understanding human nature, put the sword of the magistrate in the hand of Noah and decreed that, if a man sheds another man's blood, by other men shall that man's blood be shed.

Now the government that exists is ordained of God. According to Scripture, delegated authorities are appointed of God. That is exactly what it means. You may say to men, "But some men in places of responsibility are not godly men." The spirit of the Scripture indicates that however they may have been selected—even evil men with no thought of God—the very fact that God permits them to be in such positions indicates that God has a purpose to fulfill through their positions. They may not be godly; they may not honor God in their hearts. But God has allowed them to be there.

Men always seem to get the kind of government they deserve. We face some problems in the nation today because we deserve them! A good example is the fiasco called Watergate, an incident filled with dishonesty, disgust, shame, and indecency because our nation is filled with little Watergates! Deceit is a way of life with most of the people in this country. When God allows—I did not say he appoints—when God allows evil, ungodly men to fill places of responsibility, he does it because he uses them to correct the evil of society. You can be sure if God allows even one unregenerate person in public office, he has a purpose in it.

Nations come and go. Kingdoms rise and fall. Empires wax and wane. Behind them all is God, overruling in the affairs of men. Wars and rumors of wars, famines and pestilences, depressions and disasters; all are woven into the fabric of history. From our view the strands may seem like tangles; meaningless, hopelessly knotted, unequal and wrong. But the tapestry God is weaving is perfect and all the pressures of satanic forces in human sin are gloriously overruled by God who is omnipotent. James Russell Lowell said:

> Careless seems the great Avenger
>   history's pages but record
> One death-grapple in the darkness 'twixt
>   old systems and the Word;
> Truth forever on the scaffold,
>   Wrong forever on the throne—
> Yet the scaffold sways the future,
>   and, behind the dim unknown,
> Standeth God within the shadow,
>   keeping watch above His own.

So I declare to you again that all governmental authority exists because it is ordained of God. God is working his purpose in it; therefore, we as Christian citizens are to live in respect for that authority. There is no biblical question about that. Only seldom are Christians called upon to go against the government in order to uphold their convictions about Jesus Christ. When such occasions occur, the need may arise for us to stand for Jesus against authority. Unfortunately, however, too many of us have rationalized and only said we are standing against government because of our conviction when the truth is we have let the familiar spirit of lawlessness and contempt for authority invade our hearts. God condemns it as sin.

The second statement of Paul is that we are to acknowledge the work of rulers as being for the purpose of God. In verse 3, he admonishes "rulers are not a terror to good works." You are able to determine if your conduct is right. You don't have to look over your shoulder! I am not proud of it, but I have on occasion driven down the highways and knew I was driving too fast. So I looked over my shoulder to see if anyone was looking! What took me by surprise recently in New Mexico was that the state police were not behind me. They were above me in a helicopter! It was so easy to rationalize my action while the patrolman wrote out the citation. I complained about their unfair speed trap but the truth of the matter is, if I had been driving within the speed limit, I would not have had to worry about anything.

You see, law does not exist to punish people for doing what is right; law exists to punish those who are doing wrong. Some of you have been critical of the law and the courts, because you think you have not been given fair treatment. It may well be you are guilty of worse crimes than you have even been charged with and you know it in your heart to be true.

Don't blame the law; don't blame the government; don't rebel against authority when you have done wrong. As Christians it is not ours to decide which laws we are going to obey; it is not ours to decide whether we are going to be honest. We are commissioned of our Lord Jesus to live as respectable citizens of our country and give respect to those in authority.

Here is something else that needs to be said: "Rulers are avengers of wrath to those who do evil." One of the reasons the court systems are not punishing evil in our day is that we as citizens, having so much evil in our lives, do not have the backbone to sit on juries and render verdicts that will undergird the action police take in the streets to enforce the law. In the newspaper recently was an article about a man who had killed in cold-blooded murder seven people in this city and who later was set free to roam the streets and perhaps to kill your family or mine. The press also reported recently a similar case in which a criminal sex offender who had been convicted more than once was turned completely free and judged fit for probation in this very city!

It is the responsibility of the government to punish criminals. It is high time that we, the people, started standing behind the government and law enforcement! We can begin by saying: "Yes, put us on a jury, we will be honest. Yes, let us make the decision; we will be fair; we will not be afraid or even concerned that a lawsuit may be brought against us by some shyster lawyer who doesn't care whether his client is right or wrong." Let me reemphasize that it is the responsibility of the government to punish crime. It must be done. Do you know why we don't? It's because everyone of us has just enough crime within to make us afraid that if we speak out against somebody else, they may speak out against us.

During the Nixon administration in 1974 a Congressional committee was investigating possible impeachment proceedings against Mr. Nixon. The committee apparently decided that the President had taken two million dollars from the milk industry for his campaigning but that, since it was all politically motivated and did not violate written laws, it was, therefore, perfectly all right! One congressman not on the committee observed that the reason for the committee's decision was that the chairman himself had also received political contributions from the milk industry for his campaign!

Mercy! Can't you see that if you have your hand in the cookie jar, you can't slap your kid when he reaches his hand in there too! We need to live decently. We need to live with integrity. We need to live morally. We need to live right. When we live right, we can take a stand against what's wrong. As Christian citizens, our attitude toward higher powers is to be one of subjection because, as Paul says in verse 2, "In resisting authority, we resist God." Oh my soul! If our nation needs anything in this day, it needs a return to a respect for authority.

Young friends when you disrespect parental authority, you are not sinning against your parents so much as you are sinning against God. Christian young person, your rebellion against your parents' authority is a sin against God!

As a youth, I did some things that my dad instructed me to do when I didn't think they were right. It was proved later on rare occasions that he was wrong. That happened very few times. He had the percentages in his favor! But even when it proved he was wrong, he was still right; he was my dad. Let me tell you that we need to return to that kind of respect for authority.

We need it in the church. As your pastor, I have been appointed of God under Christ to stand on the authority of the Holy Spirit and to be the leader of this church. I didn't choose it that way; you didn't choose it that way; God did it that way. And you don't have any choice in the matter except to follow that authority. When I move out from under the hand of God, then you are to fire me. But, you must fire me or follow me; you don't have any other choices. The same principle applies to our church staff. I caution you against criticizing my helpers. They are in spiritual authority in this church. God put them there.

Do not go home and have fried preacher on Sunday afternoon and then wonder why your children don't respect their teachers. Don't you understand what they are learning at home? Did you ever hear that silly little song:

> Listen to the children while they play,
> Ain't it kind of funny what the children say.

You know, "Skip a Rope." You hear children repeat things they hear about cheating on taxes; and "Mommy hates Daddy, and Daddy hates Mom." What the children say is not very funny because they learn it from us.

As Christians we are to respect authority—authority in the home, authority in the church, authority in the school, authority in the government. Oh God, deliver us from the anti-authoritanian, rebellious spirit of this age. Nothing in our society is worse than the piggish attitude of the person who says: "I don't have to pay any attention to anybody; it's my life and I'm going to live it; it's my thing and I'm going to do it." If you feel that way, get out of society. Go off into the mountains, be a hermit, and do your thing by yourself. But don't impose it on somebody else.

We are to be subject to authority because resisters will receive judgment, the apostle Paul says in verse 2. He says again in verse 3 that the ones doing good need not fear because they will be praised by the authorities. Resisters are subject to evil. They have reason to be afraid but those who do what is right have no reason for fear. He says in verse 5 that the Christian should be subject to authority simply for conscience sake. In other words, obey civil authorities because it's right. No other reason is needed. In verse 7, he advises that this includes paying taxes and giving respect to everyone who deserves respect as well as those in authority. The things we learn from the Scripture are Paul's instructions to Christian citizens. We are to live with respect for our fellowmen, respect for God, and respect for government. We are to live disciplined, respectful lives and thereby bring glory to the Lord Christ.

To this point, you have probably assessed Paul's instructions as essential but practically impossible to completely follow. Taking Paul seriously means you've accepted a pretty big assignment—too big, in fact, to be carried out in purely human strength. So look with me now to verses 8-10 and you will see our inspiration. In this brief passage, Paul gives the one secret for keeping the law. He says that love is the fulfillment of all laws. He who loves his neighbor will seek diligently not to violate love's trustful relationship. The Christian does not need to seek a legal relationship with his neighbor. To recall all written laws in order to obey them in reference to a neighbor would be a tedious task, taxing the Christian's patience without producing any worthwhile results. But Paul assures us that love will not violate any law. Love never works a hardship on anyone else. Love is the fulfillment of the law. So, what is he saying? He is saying we can live the prescribed way because our rebellious hearts have been conquered by the love of the Lord Jesus Christ.

Now Paul says in verse 8 that love's debt is to owe no man anything except to love one another. What does he mean? He advises us not to go in debt for what we cannot pay. No restriction is intended on buying needed goods through loans. It is a teaching against borrowing what we cannot repay, against living beyond your means. To buy something you know you cannot pay for is as much stealing as if you picked the article from the shelf and walked unobserved out of the store.

Paul said further that there is one debt you can never repay and that is the debt of love. So he said you need to be in love's debt to every man. You need to love all people even as Christ loved us and gave himself for us.

In verse 9, he tells of love's duty. Jesus reduced the commandments to two: Thou shalt love the Lord thy God and thy neighbor as thyself. Paul declares that, if you keep those two commandments, the intent of the law will have been fulfilled. In verse 10, he tells us love's desire is for the well-being of our fellowman and to be well-pleasing to God. The motivation for it all comes from living under the inspiration of Christian love as we experience it in our Lord Jesus Christ. Do that and you will have no problem being subject to governmental authority, being subject to God's authority, and living among your fellowman as a Christian ought so to do.

Finally, in verses 11-14, Paul speaks of our incentive. He

first gave us our instruction. Then he showed us our inspiration. Now in verses 11 and following, he shows our incentive for good citizenship is that we are about to step into the eternal glories. We are nearer to Jesus than when we first believed. Therefore we ought to journey in the light of our eternal home. We must live with reference to our eternal salvation.

Our Lord Jesus Christ would say to us, "I am coming soon. You are to live with respect for authority. Perhaps living under the authority of evil men seems occasionally more than you can bear but, after all, you will have to endure it only a little while. Some day soon you will come to live with me in eternity." Paul echoes the same encouragement, saying that we are to endure hardness as good soldiers of Jesus Christ in order to bring honor and glory to his name.

In verse 11, Paul advises us to watch viligantly for the coming of Christ. Verse 12 says we are to war valiantly against sin until he comes. Verse 13 says we are to walk virtuously and verse 14 says we are to wait victoriously, claiming that the flesh should have no allowance in our lives because our Lord Jesus Christ has already gone to the cross. It was there he conquered sin, death, and evil. He has arisen from the grave. He is coming again. The victory is ours. It is secure. It is complete, and we can live as godly citizens in an ungodly world, knowing that our salvation is nearer than when we first believed.

I say to you on the basis of God's Word that there is no such thing as a Christian who has a rebellious heart against authority. There is no such thing as a person living close to God who has an antiauthoritarian spirit. If at this moment, your heart is in a turmoil of rebellion and antiauthoritarianism; if you find yourself constantly doing battle with authority; and if you do not have respect for those around you, it is a clear indication that you either have never been to the cross to be washed in the blood of Jesus or you have wandered so far away from that place of commitment until the love of the Lord Jesus Christ has waned cold in your heart.

Do you know what you need to do? You need to come to the cross. You need to bow at the foot of that cross where all rebellion, resentment, indecency, and immorality can be washed from your soul and the loving Lord Jesus Christ can enter and set up his residence in your heart so that you might be able to live among men as God's man ought so to live. Why don't you come to Jesus? Let his authority conquer your soul, and you'll find respect for authority is a simple matter of Christian response to the Lord Jesus.

Luke 7:41-48

There was a certain creditor which had two debtors: the one owed five hundred pence, and the other fifty.

And when they had nothing to pay, he frankly forgave them both. Tell me therefore, which of them will love him most?

And Simon answered and said, I suppose that he, to whom he forgave most. And he said unto him, Thou hast rightly judged.

And he turned to the woman, and said unto Simon, Seest thou this woman? I entered into thine house, thou gavest me no water for my feet: but she hath washed my feet with tears, and wiped them with the hairs of her head.

Thou gavest me no kiss: but this woman since the time I came in hath not ceased to kiss my feet.

My head with oil thou didst not anoint: but this woman hath anointed my feet with ointment.

Wherefore I say unto thee, Her sins, which are many, are forgiven; for she loved much: but to whom little is forgiven, the same loveth little.

And he said unto her, Thy sins are forgiven.

8
The High Cost of Free Forgiveness

On a battlefield in France in 1918, Sergeant-Major
Robert S. McCormick was instrumental in saving the life of
his commanding officer, Major Harry Parkin. Every year
thereafter, for at least twenty-five years. on the anniversary
of that occasion Mr. Parkin wrote a letter to express his gratitude to the man who had saved his life. In 1943, in the
twenty-fifth of those annual letters, Mr. Parkin wrote:

> Dear Bob:
>   I again want to express to you my appreciation for
> another year of life which I could not ordinarily have
> enjoyed had it not been for you and the price you were
> willing to pay to save my life. I want you to know I
> am grateful.

Freedom is never free. That is a paradoxical statement,
and yet it will stand up. For you see, freedom never comes
without a price. No one has ever experienced freedom for
which someone has not paid. Freedom is retained by a similar price that many must pay to uphold it day by day. If
freedom is to be retained, freedom must be coveted by all
of those who experience and enjoy it. You and I as citizens
of the United States of America, in spite of all our problems,

difficulties, and criticisms, should stand today to express gratitude because of the freedom we have and the price that has purchased that freedom.

Our paradox has an interesting corollary. Just as it is true that freedom is not free, in the same manner we come to say that forgiveness is never free. Now a person might say: "Pastor, forgiveness must be free or it becomes recompense rather than forgiveness, If a person has to purchase forgiveness, it is not really forgiveness but recompense for his deed." This may be true to an extent, but the point I am making is simply this: Forgiveness always is a costly thing. There never has been an occasion when a parent has forgiven a disobedient child that it did not exact a price from the parent in love, tears, heartbreak, and terrible strife within his soul. Even though forgiveness may seem to be freely imparted through a simple pronouncement, forgiveness never is really free.

Our text is a parabolic illustration found in Luke 7. Jesus gave the parable on the occasion of his visit in the home of one of the Pharisees. Much is said in the Bible about God's free forgiveness. I believe there is more truth contained in what Jesus has to say in this parable than perhaps many of us have been able to see. Observing today's circumstances, we see in the parabolic teaching of our Lord just what forgiveness really is. The Scripture relates how forgiveness comes and what kind of response forgiveness from sin prompts in the hearts of those who are forgiven.

In order to understand any story better, we need to understand the circumstance—the situation that surrounds it—and how the story came to be used. Keep in mind the fact that a parable is a true-to-life story. It is not necessarily an incident that actually occurred. The story has, however, all the elements of normal life situations and was used by the Lord to reveal eternal truths about God.

The occasion for the parable is an invitation to Jesus from one of the most religious men of his day. The Bible says a Pharisee named Simon was the one who invited Jesus into his home. We must understand that this is an unusual situation because most of the Pharisees considered Jesus their enemy. They were confronted by him; they felt threatened by him, because Jesus brought a new kind of understanding of God. The Pharisees had been able to keep the people wrapped up in their legalism and in their religiosity. Now Jesus was saying that a man's relationship to God depended upon his own personal faith.

The Pharisees normally were the enemies of Christ. There were occasions, however, when some of them listened to him and many of them showed some sympathy with his teaching. Whatever may be the reason, Jesus is found to have accepted the hospitality of a Pharisee of his time. The man's name was Simon and Jesus went into his home. Nothing is said about Simon having extended to Jesus any of the common courtesies normally expected in a visit to a prominent Eastern home of that time. According to custom, Simon would have had a basin of water and would have had a servant there to wash Jesus' feet. The people walked on dusty desert roads; they wore open-toed sandals; their feet were often hot and soiled from the blazing sun and sand. So, a common custom was to provide a household slave to wash the feet of guests.

In this instance, the custom was foregone; it did not take place as usual. Not only so, but normally a man would have been received with a customary kiss of greeting. That also was foregone. Another of the social amenities omitted was the application of cooling ointments and oils for anointing a guest's head. All of these things were passed over. The Bible simply indicates that Simon the Pharisee had invited Jesus in, and he sat down to meat.

Now, a strange thing happened. Luke says that a woman, a sinner, entered into Simon's house and began to show devotion to Jesus. The word sinner is a synonym for harlot. The woman was a prostitute, a woman of the streets. She entered across Simon the Pharisee's threshold and came to Jesus and began to weep over his feet. As she wept, the tears fell on his feet. She kissed his feet and dried them with the hair of her head. Her next act was not to take some precious ointment and pour it on his head, but instead, to take costly ointment and anoint the feet of the Lord Jesus Christ.

This put Simon in an unusual position. He could not understand what was happening. In the first place, he probably was aghast that a woman of the streets would be so brazen as to enter his home. Simon would consider himself a very good, fine, upstanding man in the community. You need never think that he had ever met this woman before. A man like Simon—cold, dispassionate, self-righteous— never would have been approached by a woman of her kind at any time. So Simon's mind began to go to work in ways like so many of us. He thought he could judge the situation by what he knew of people. He knew that this woman was a woman of the street. He was acquainted with the kind of person she was, so immediately he began to judge her attention to Jesus in the terms of passion and of the flesh.

Not only did Simon judge, but he also began to evaluate the Lord in terms of what he knew about the woman. Simon, in his self-righteous, hypocritical nature, took inventory of the situation and began to judge the Son of God—the Lord Jesus Christ. Simon said: "If Jesus had been a prophet, he would know what kind of woman it was that was touching him, and he would have cast her out of His presence." Jesus perceived Simon's attitude and that became the occasion for the parable. Jesus was ready to teach Simon a lesson about the forgiving grace of God.

A very interesting insight into the Scripture is that Jesus had already met this woman. It is quite evident from the language of the text that she had come to Jesus previously and met him somewhere out in public. Jesus had forgiven her sins and she had become a devoted disciple. She had come to Simon's house because of the appreciation she felt for Christ. Jesus knew the woman; Simon only thought he knew her. Jesus accepted her devotion on the basis of what he, as the Son of God, knew to be in her heart. So Jesus addressed this parable to Simon.

Jesus said: "Simon, suppose there were two men who owed a debt to one moneylender. One of them owed him fifty pence: the other owed him five hundred pence." Do not try to translate the sums into American dollars. The important matter is that both of them owed him, and one of them owed him ten times as much as the other. If you should wish to understand how much it might have been, a penny in that day was a day's wages. In today's vastly inflated economy, it would still be representative of an average day's pay. One man owed him five hundred days' work, and the other man owed him fifty days' work. Five hundred days—that is just short of two years! It was a total of probably about two working years that one man was in debt to him. Both of the men owed the same creditor, and neither of them could pay.

Jesus said: "Simon, he frankly forgave them both, he just wiped out the debt; he counted it as null and void, and neither owed him anything." Simon was shocked. He just could not figure out anybody ever doing that—just letting a man completely out of debt and not exercising his prerogative to collect it! Jesus said: "Simon, he simply forgave them both. Now Simon, which one of these men would appreciate most the forgiveness of the debt?" Simon began to see some application to the story. He began to see that Jesus was pointedly saying something about the situation involving himself and the sinful woman. Simon would admit, as a Pharisee, that he was a sinner, but he never would admit he was as much a sinner as the woman. So Simon answered, "I would assume the one who was forgiven the most."

You and I know that many other things are implied in the parable, but for the moment, Jesus accepted Simon's answer. He said, "That's right." The point he was trying to get across is simply this: "Simon, to whom much is forgiven, there will be much love and much appreciation shown." Jesus was saying in other words, that the person who is forgiven most will be most appreciative.

What was Jesus really saying? The man who is most conscious of his sin and the most conscious of his need for forgiveness, the man who remembers best his indebtedness is the man who is most appreciative of its being written off. So we come to see that this is the circumstance. The main teaching of the parable is that the man who is most aware and most conscious of his position before God as a sinner, is the man who will be most grateful for salvation and forgiveness that God offers in Jesus Christ.

There are three statements I want to make about this

parable and about this situation. They are very simple, and I think you will be able to see something in them that will help you.

The first thing is this: I believe that Jesus is showing us that all men are spiritually in debt. Jesus said there was a moneylender and two men owed money. Now, granted, one owed him ten times as much as the other, but they both owed him money. Many of us understand something about owing money. I could preach about a lot of things and some would say, "Now, I don't know anything about that." On some occasions you could possibly say: "I went to church this morning and the pastor preached out of the Bible about things I had never heard of, and I just did not understand any of it." Well, friend, I am talking about owing money right now and I doubt there is anyone who doesn't understand what I am talking about! Both men owed the man money. They both understood their indebtedness.

The question Jesus voiced was this: "Which will love the most—which one will be most appreciative?" The answer the Pharisee gave is the one Jesus accepted for application of the moment. The truth of the matter is, when it comes to debt and the forgiveness, no man can dare limit his memory. There is much that a good memory will do to prompt realization of and appreciation for the debts we owe and the price that has been paid. So often we as citizens of our country take for granted the freedoms that are ours. We never quite appreciate the price that someone has paid for those freedoms. I get a bit weary when veterans, for instance, march on the Capitol of the United States. They think because they are veterans of one war they can obliterate all that has been established by many veterans who

gave their lives and are not alive to demonstrate. Often mis-
guided men stalk up and down the Capitol lawn and say,
"We're going to close down the government until we get
what we want." If you want to close down the government,
my question is, "Who is going to pay your veterans' benefits and who is going to pay the welfare checks?" We *are*
the government, and we had better remember with some
respect and appreciation that freedom is a privilege which
has been secured by the sacrifice of many. It does not give
a man the right to trample on everybody who has paid the
price for his freedom for over two hundred years just because he fought in Vietnam. I have no personal vendetta
at this point. I am just making a statement of personal
conviction. A man needs to have an excellent memory if
he is going to be appreciative of his freedoms and the resulting debts he owes.

The same is also very true when it comes to forgiveness
of sin. Simon was a man who would say: "Well, now after
all, God's pretty fortunate to have me on his team, because
I don't do this and I don't do that." Simon seemed to
look upon God as some kind of an investor. He would say,
"God, I've got a good thing going if you want to put a little
money into it." Simon had forgotten that he was by nature
a sinner. Simon also appeared to have overlooked the fact
that the sins of the spirit are more distasteful in the sight
of God than the sins of the flesh. I dare say that if Jesus
had made the application of who was a five hundred-times
sinner and who was a fifty-times sinner, it might surprise
you, as well as Simon, to know that the righteous, religious
Pharisee might have been the greater sinner in the sight of
God. God gets sick of pride, self-righteousness, and high-
headedness in those who think they are something so special

that God is lucky to have them aboard.

Whether you are a person of the streets or a picture of beautiful character in your community, it will do you well to remember the sin that has separated you from God and that all of us are in debt because of our sin. We are in debt unto God. We have a sin debt that must be paid and we must face that fact. Society is in debt to God for the redemption revealed in Jesus Christ. Not all of society has been saved, but all of society has been affected by redemption in Christ. All of the world is better off because Jesus Christ lived. He came to redeem all of the world, and he is ultimately some day going to redeem all of the world when he comes again. Not every individual in the world, but those who trust him, shall participate in that redemption. Nevertheless, all men are affected by that redemption and the world stands in debt to God for it.

We who are Christians are in debt to God for our salvation. Lest we become high-minded and heady, lest we get enamored with ourselves, lest we start enjoying our little fellowship of faith too much and stop reaching out to a lost and dying world, let me remind you with the apostle Paul: we are debtors unto all men. God has granted to us and entrusted to us the saving gospel of Jesus Christ and, therefore, we are in debt to the world and we share it with them. Ours is the debt of a Louis Pasteur, the French chemist whose research resulted in immense medical benefits for mankind everywhere; ours is the debt of a Jonas Salk who developed the famous vaccine for the dread polio. We must share what we have found in Christ. We are in debt to God for redemption and in debt to a lost world that needs our Lord and his redemption.

The second thing I want to point out is this: None of us

can pay. Notice what the parable related: Jesus said there was a certain moneylender. He lent money to two fellows. Neither one of them could pay. In principle, that made the debts equal. If a debtor cannot pay, what difference does it make how much he owes? He cannot be put any further into jail for owing five million than for owing five hundred. When he cannot pay—he cannot pay.

I do not know your situation. I do not know if your life has been couched in immorality. I do not know if the filth of the world has touched you or not. You may be the best person in your community in your opinion and perhaps in your neighbors' opinions. You may be a gutter bum, a drunkard on the streets, or a prostitute in a flop house. I do not know where you are or who you are but, when it comes to standing before God in our natural state without Jesus Christ, all of us are in debt in sin and none of us can pay.

Sin debt cannot be paid by moral attainment. If that were possible, Simon could have paid. Morally, he had attained a good standing. Simon was a good man, a respected man. If moral attainment will take care of sin, then Simon would have been paid up. Moral attainment will not do it.

Loving devotion will not do it. The woman came in, she washed Jesus' feet, and she wiped them with her hair. Perhaps someone would say: "The way to be forgiven then is to do things that seem to be humiliating. The way to be forgiven is to bow before God and to be very pious and meek." Let me assure you that the woman was not forgiven because she washed Jesus' feet. In Greek, the language in which the New Testament was written, the verbs of the text are perfect tense, which denote completed action. The expression actually means, "Thy sins have been forgiven."

On every occasion in which Jesus speaks of the woman's forgiveness, he says, "Your sins already have been forgiven." The reason was that she had met Jesus earlier. She had already found forgiveness of her sin. She had already received the free peace of God in her heart. Now she had come, not to receive forgiveness, but to show her loving devotion. She had a good memory of her own sin, the debt that had been paid in her behalf, and the forgiveness she had received through Jesus.

You are never going to be able to be good enough or work hard enough to wash away your sin debt. When you come to Jesus Christ and in him find your sin debt paid, your heart should be so full of the memory of what he has done for you that you will want to serve him out of love.

The last point is this; namely, that all men are sinners. No man can pay, but forgiveness is available to all. Forgiveness is costly, never free, but the price has already been paid. What did it cost the creditor in the parable to forgive the debts of two men? His kindness cost him five hundred days' work from one man and fifty days' work from the other. That is all it cost and, in truth, that is not a great deal. It cost him something, however, because he gave up the services owed him. Perhaps his loss was doubled if he had to hire someone else to perform the required labor. If it were necessary for him to go do the work himself, then perhaps he had to leave other things undone. It cost the man something to forgive. It always costs something to forgive.

You know nothing about the high cost of free forgiveness until you understand what it cost God to cancel your sin debt. The only claim you and I have on God is on his heart, mercy, and grace. We have no claim on God because of our goodness. We have no claim on God because of our righteousness. The only claim we have on God rests on his love. God's love, grace, and mercy never operate at the expense of God's holiness. In keeping with his holiness and righteousness, God decreed that, if man sins, man shall die. Death is the penalty for sin. Before God would forgive your sin debt, somebody had to pay the penalty. That is what it cost God, the cross of Jesus Christ. That is where the cross comes in. That is what the death of Jesus means. In order for God to be true to his own holy nature, his only begotten Son—the best that heaven had to give—came to the earth, suffered the agonies of life, was persecuted by men like you and me, and died on a Roman cross, condemned as a criminal. He died to pay the sin debt of you and me.

You are a debtor. You owe a sin debt. Your greatest need is to be forgiven of your sin. You may successfully fool your wife, your husband, or your children, but you do not have to try to fool me. I am a man and, therefore, I know what it is to bear unforgiven guilt. I know what it is to wake up at two o'clock in the morning with my conscience eating away at me and my heart bursting out of my body. I know something else—there is no way you can forgive yourself, and there is no price you can pay to take care of that guilt. Let me tell you something. I brought my sin debt to Calvary's cross and knelt at the feet of the Lord Jesus Christ. In his precious blood I felt my sins washed away. I once was blind but now I see; I once was in debt but now I am free.

You are a debtor. You can never pay. Jesus has already paid the price for your costly but free forgiveness, if you will accept him today.

I am told that in the country of France the graves of soldiers are marked by simple little wooden crosses. The women of France have volunteered to take care of those graves. The way a woman signifies the acceptance of her responsibility for keeping one grave site clean is that she writes on a little cross, "I accept," and she signs her name. That is the way your sin debt will be paid if it is ever paid. You must go to the cross of Jesus, open your heart and say, "Lord, I accept, I accept." Will you do it?

Psalm 33:12-22

Blessed is the nation whose God is the Lord; and the people whom he hath chosen for his own inheritance.

The Lord looketh from heaven; he beholdeth all the sons of men.

From the place of his habitation he looketh upon all the inhabitants of the earth.

He fashioned their hearts alike; he considereth all their works.

There is no king saved by the multitude of an host: a mighty man is not delivered by much strenth.

An horse is a vain thing for safety: neither shall he deliver any by his great strength.

Behold, the eye of the Lord is upon them that fear him, upon them that hope in his mercy.

To deliver their soul from death, and to keep them alive in famine.

Our soul waiteth for the Lord: he is our help and our shield.

For our heart shall rejoice in him, because we have trusted in his holy name.

Let thy mercy, O Lord, be upon us, according as we hope in thee.

Blessed Is the Nation

The history of America has been written in the ink of her involvement with God. His blessings abound upon this nation in a marvelous manner. It seems that from the day of her founding, until this good day, God has held America in his hand in an unusual way.

America grew great because America was built on the Christian foundation. When the Pilgrims landed at Plymouth, they knelt to thank God for this new land. The church of the Lord Jesus Christ was the center of each new settlement. Our government was born with a call to prayer when Benjamin Franklin stopped the deliberations of the Continental Congress to kneel and pray for divine guidance.

There have been other nations that have risen to power and prominence. The Medo-Persians had a great nation, but they drank their way to death. Egypt flourished under Joseph, but after four hundred years, they forgot him and his God, and Egypt erupted in chaotic confusion. Alexander the Great conquered the world but could not control himself and died a defeated man in a drunken orgy. His kingdom was dispersed in dissipation. Rome became the proud ruler of the world, but lust and luxury leveled her to insignificance in world affairs.

In contrast to many others, America is a nation which
has been built on "the better." Because of her recognition
of God's provision, America's resources are resounding. The
Creator has given us bountiful natural beauty, freedom from
oppression, relative religious liberties, and many other blessings. Surely, we can say with the psalmist, "Blessed is the
nation whose God is the Lord."

Yet, in spite of these blessings, our nation knows need.
After two hundred years, we are in a state of moral collapse
and spiritual bankruptcy. In 1960 only one of the 115
deaths in the city of Chicago was by homicide. In 1974 the
figure was one of 35. We experience five times more violent
crimes per capita than any other nation in the world. There
have been more murders in our history than deaths in all
the wars we have fought. The number of births is bested by
the abortions in some of our largest cities.

The *Reader's Digest* of April, 1974, stated, "According
to the National Institute on Alcohol Abuse and Alocholism,
1.3 million Americans between twelve and seventeen years
of age have serious drinking problems. About one third of
our high school students confess to getting drunk at least
once a month. Arrests for teenage drunk driving have
tripled since 1960. Sixty percent of all people killed in
drunken driving accidents are now in their teens."

Twenty-five percent of our people are involved in the
occult in some form, desperately trying to find meaning
and purpose in life. Someone has said that the crisis in our
age is not a political but a moral crisis. It is a crisis of people who have given up their hope in God.

All of these things point us to our need to pause, yea,
even stop where we are to see how Americans have been
blessed and what America must do again to know the bene-

fit of being "God's chosen." The text before us from the Psalms calls us to consider the answer.

Psalm 33 is a triumphant song of praise which opens with a call for music. All modes of expression are summoned to service: "rejoice," "praise," "give thanks," "sing," "play instruments." In verses 4-11 the praise proceeds as Jehovah is extolled for his greatness and goodness. His Word is right, his work is faithful as we see in verse 4. Verse 5 shows us that his character is perfect, mingled with light. Righteousness and judgment are mingled amid love. His lovingkindness is bestowed upon men. In verses 6-9 we read that he has created all things, and the conclusion of verses 10-11 is that he overrules in the affairs of men.

As a people then acknowledge God, those chosen of him for his glory are given to praise. He chose Israel, and in their interest he watches all the sons of men, as verses 12-15 declare. His watchfulness of his people is a greater security than armies of men with horses and chariots. This is presented in verses 16-19. The chorus of praise climaxes with an affirmative of trust and assurance of joy and a prayer for mercy in verse 22.

Our consideration for now is centered in verse 12, "Blessed is the nation whose God is the Lord." America and Americans have been bountifully blessed. Yet, we see these blessings being bartered away by the merchants of sin and unbelief. We pray, "God bless America," knowing that in him is our hope. When the individual moves to Christ, his personal liberty is established. When a nation kneels at his feet, its blessings are certain.

The nation that knows the blessing of God is one whose strength is secure. The strength of any country is in the quality of her people. The strength of any person is in the character of his being. Where does a people and where do persons find strength for living?

We in America have tried many things. We have pursued personal pleasure until our entertainment budget far outdistances that of any other nation. Our insatiable thirst for knowledge has made us first among all in inventions and science. We have run after wealth until we are the richest country in the history of the world. Our armaments programs have pushed us to an unparalleled position of military power. In spite of all of these, we are a frightened people. We shudder at the sign of war in spite of our warring instruments. In my own lifetime we have fought three wars. One of these wars we won, only to lessen the victory by acknowledging those who acknowledged not God. The next war in Korea was a never-won war, which still smacks of an uncertain settlement. The last conflict we lost. Take it any way you want, in Vietnam, we lost. Obviously, our ships, planes, missiles, spacecraft, and all armaments aren't answer enough. How could we possibly lose with all of these instruments when our forefathers won without any of them?

Surely it should be clearly seen, the strength of a people is not in her military might, nor is the strength of a person in his own power. The strength of a people is in dependence upon God. It is he who ordains in the affairs of men. So long as a nation remains godly, she remains great. So long as an individual is filled with God's presence, that individual remains victorious. We must move to the place where we again truly look to God.

Neither America nor Americans shall ever stand certain of sufficient strength for all challenges until we stand in the might of his divine majesty. Our rulers need to remember, "He removeth kings, and setteth up kings" (Dan. 2:21). The

Most High rules in the kingdoms of men and sits up over it the basest of men.

The powers that be are ordained of God. God has even used the ungodly to work his purpose. Hitler, the mass murderer of Europe will someday be revealed as an instrument in the hands of God to work his ultimate purpose.

The psalmist, warrior and writer, knew what he was talking about, for although he became a great king, he was yet severely punished for numbering his soldiers, thereby indicating that deliverance from his enemies was wholly dependent upon a brave host of men. God has never promised to be on the side of big battalions. National security is not the outcome of strong fighting forces alone or possession of the most deadly weapons. No country is immune from defeat because of its possessions. As Isaiah said: "Woe to them that go down to Egypt for help; and stay on horses, and trust in chariots, because they are many; and in horsemen because they are very strong; but they look not unto the Holy One of Israel, neither seek the Lord" (Isa. 31:1).

The psalmist declared, "Some trust in chariots, and some in horses, but we will remember the name of the Lord our God" (Ps. 20:7).

Napoleon led more than one-half million men into Russia, but the terrible winter left the army a wreck, and soon their general was a lone POW on St. Helena. All along through history, this is verified. As the great man of the pulpit Charles Hadden Spurgeon once said, "The strongest battalions melt like snowflakes when God is against them."

American strength is marvelous. It has been built by a tradition of men of character and faith. In these moments when a trembling is felt we need to be the people "whose God is the Lord." In him there is sufficiency of strength which brings security.

Blessed is the nation who has claimed the provision that is promised. In verses 18-19 of Psalm 33, we see that men are ever under the watchful eye of God. As we fear him, we can rely upon his steady love. Then comes the clear promise, "He will keep them from death even in the time of famine."

Our world is fast becoming a scene of shortages. Those of us in America have experienced it only by leaving off a little luxury. The world as a whole has felt the strain in the hunger haunts of stomachs which are seldom satisfied. This is not necessary. God has promised plentious provision throughout his Word to all of those who are his by response to his elective grace. In another place, the psalmist wrote, "I have been young and now am old; yet have I not seen the righteous forsaken, nor his seed begging bread" (Ps. 37:25). And again he says, "Trust in the Lord . . . and verily thou shalt be fed." (Ps. 37:3). The wisdom writer stated, "The righteous eateth to the satisfying of his soul" (Prov. 13:25). Through the prophet Joel came the promise, "Ye shall eat in plenty and be satisfied" (Joel 2:26). Certainly the promise reached its pinnacle when from the mouth of our Lord came the words, "Seek ye first the kingdom of God and his righteousness, and all of these things shall be added unto you."

Certainly the same God who in his Son Jesus has taught us to pray for "our daily bread" is able in that same Christ "to provide all our needs." Blessed is the nation who pauses for her provision, not from the hand of a welfare government, but from the bounty of a merciful creator.

Blessed is the nation whose people have realized a certain salvation. In verses 20-22 of our text, the psalmist speaks of the greatest gift. He has already said, "Blessed is the na-

tion whose God is the Lord." Now he teaches us that those
who wait upon the Lord shall rejoice in him because
through trust in God by his Son Jesus Christ there comes
certain salvation.

The song ends with an affirmation of trust. Our nation
was born by faith in God. On the first coin that was ever
minted in America, there was a picture of Moses. Even today, the money, after which we so madly run, reminds us
to trust in God. From this trust flows an assurance of joy.
As *The Living Bible, Paraphrased* states it, "No wonder we
are happy in the Lord." The heaviness of soul which hangs
its dark shadow over our nation could be removed and we
could be a people of joy if only we could come again to
bask in the sunlight of belief. The churches of God, yea, the
children of God, are blessed with abundant joy when they
trust in the Lord.

When we learn to trust God and give our lives to his Son
Jesus Christ, we shall live in joy with the prayerful dependence on God's love to surround us. God must deal with
all nations, either in judgment or blessing. So must each
individual do business with his God. As we come to trust
in him for salvation, as the church of our Lord Jesus shakes
from its slumbers, we shall be able to sing with renewed
confidence "God Bless America."

Blessed is the nation whose God is the Lord. Blessed is
the individual whose Savior is Jesus Christ. As you would
seek for freedom today, from the sin that besets your soul,
let me remind you that its price has been paid and no little
price it was, for on the cross Jesus Christ gave himself that
you might be free from the law of sin and death. If you
will give yourself to him, he will save you today; and if we
who are saved will give ourselves to serving him, he will

again lead this nation to experience that joy of being
blessed indeed.

"What Makes a Nation Great"

Not serried ranks with flags unfurled,
Not armored ships that gird the world,
Not hoarded wealth nor busy mills,
Not cattle on a thousand hills,
Not sages wise, nor schools nor laws,
Nor boasted deeds in freedom's cause—
All these may be, and yet the state
In the eye of God be far from great.

That land is great which knows the Lord,
Whose songs are guided by His Word;
Where justice rules 'twixt man and man,
Where love controls in art and plan;
Where, breathing in his native air,
Each soul find joy in praise and prayer—
Thus may our country good and great,
Be God's delight—man's estate.

Alexander Blackburn

Matthew 16:13-20

When Jesus came into the coasts of Caesarea Phillipi, he asked his disciples, saying, Whom do men say that I the Son of man am?

And they said, Some say that thou art John the Baptist: some Elias; and others, Jeremias, or one of the prophets.

He saith unto them, But whom say ye that I am?

And Simon Peter answered and said, Thou art the Christ, the Son of the living God.

And Jesus answered and said unto him, Blessed art thou, Simon Bar-jona: for flesh and blood hath not revealed it unto thee, but my Father which is in heaven.

And I say also unto thee, That thou art Peter, and upon this rock I will build my church; and the gates of hell shall not prevail against it.

And I will give unto thee the keys of the kingdom of heaven: and whatsoever thou shalt bind on earth shall be bound in heaven: and whatsoever thou shalt loose on earth shall be loosed in heaven.

Then charged he his disciples that they should tell no man that he was Jesus the Christ.

10
Freedom Through the Church

As we have opportunity to turn our thoughts to the abundant heritage which is ours as Americans; as we are being reminded repeatedly of the natural resources, material assets and political freedoms which have been handed us; it is good that we should remind ourselves of the spiritual heritage which is ours in this country.

The freedom of America has been made rich by the contribution of the church. The Christian heritage is woven into our very national existence. All competent historians will align in agreement that the influence of the Christian church has been significant and enduring. This of course is not a matter for sectarian pride. It is simply a recognition and acceptance of facts as they stand. The role of the Christian church and the past of our nation reminds us of the tremendous responsibilities that are ours for freedom in the present and in the future.

The primary purpose for looking at the past is always that we might turn our faces to the future. We have a noble heritage as Americans and as Christians living in America. It is our responsibility to preserve and perpetuate this heritage while we punctuate it with a Christian witness and principles. As we recognize our freedoms anew and afresh, let us be re-

minded that freedom comes through the church of the Lord
Jesus Christ.

As dramatic as was the day of our declaration of independence, the drama of that day can never match the intensity
of Christ's interview with his disciples at Caesarea Philippi.
As our Scripture text unfolds, we see that the setting was
scattered with religious and political associations. The
glitter from the white marble temple dedicated to the deity
which was Caesar was shadowed but by the fourteen or
more edificies of ancient Syrian Baal worship which stood
nearby. The nectar of nature worship flowed from a deep
cavern close at hand which was said to be the birthplace of
Pan, and some would say the sound of Jordan's bubbling beginning could be heard in that same cavern. In this unlikely place, where the restrictions of religious superstition
and political oppression filled the very air, the homeless,
penniless Galilean asked the twelve ordinary traveling com-
panions a searching question and fully expected a Spirit-
inspired response.

Couched in this conversation at Caesarea is counsel for
us as we would let Christ's freedom ring through the church
and its outstretching arms in this day of renewed dedica-
tion in our country. Some truths are treated in this text
which we must comprehend if we are to be the voice of
freedom through the church triumphant in our time.

In order for us to be effective in bringing spiritual freedom through the church, we must have a doctrinal direction which derives from a definite knowledge of who Jesus
is and what is his purpose upon this earth. In effect, what
Jesus said to these men was: "What is the result of my ministry up to now? How do men evaluate me? Who do they
say that I am?" Our Lord was not searching for informa-

tion. He was fully aware of what was being said about him. It was, I believe, his purpose to bring them to an understanding of who he is and what he had come to accomplish.

Their reply shows that his own age had reached some remarkable conclusions concerning Christ. Some had said he was John the Baptist, others Elijah, still others said Jeremiah or one of the prophets. There was a wide variety of opinions concerning Jesus and his mission. It seemed that men were saying: "We cannot place him, there is something of the tears of compassionate Jeremiah. We see the flame of Mount Carmel flashing in his eyes. The reformation of the Baptist seems to ring in his voice. Yet there comes the lovely lullaby of Zephaniah's song." Yes, men had trouble knowing just who Jesus was and, therefore, were confused as to his purpose.

It is so much the same today. The unregenerate world cannot comprehend him at all, and it seems tragically true that many who say, "Lord, Lord," scarcely imagine his mission. See Jesus as he narrows the inquiry to his own. "Who say ye that I am?" In Peter's inspired response is our needed identification and direction.

"Thou art the Christ." That's it! Jesus is the Anointed One who has come to deliver. Peter knew this only by inspiration, if you please, by revelation. A great problem of our day is that many want to see Jesus as a reformer, a social reactionary, an ethical teacher, or a compassionate benefactor. He is these, but he is not primarily these. He has come to accomplish multitudes of missions, but all are "spin-offs" of the primary purpose, the redemption of man from sin. Only as we allow the Holy Spirit to assure us of his identity and purpose can we be involved in his victory.

Christ has come to set men free from sin. Freedom

among nations of men will come when individual men are set free in Jesus Christ. The church is to be the voice of freedom. Freedom comes to the church as the church alines itself with a sovereign purpose of God.

The stream of God's sovereignty flows in the riverbed of redemption. If we would be swept in that stream, we must not stand on the bank and try to detour the current's direction. We must step into the stream and be a part of that purpose. A lady once said to me after my prayer for God's blessing at a ground-breaking: "Pastor Jackson, I am glad you came to pray. We will do all right if we can just get God on our side." That was what the Pharisees of the New Testament times were trying, the manipulation of divine direction. We need not to try to get the Lord on our side; we must, rather, find out what he is up to and by faith align ourselves with his sovereign purpose of deliverance, and thus the church will be again the voice of freedom to a world in bondage.

Another interesting emphasis issues from this interview. When Jesus had asked the question concerning himself, he made no more inquiries but stated facts. The first fact concerns our identity. Jesus said to Peter in effect, "Now that the Spirit has revealed this to you as to who I am, I want to tell you who you are." He went on to say, "You are Peter, a piece of rock." Why would he say such? I believe it was so that Peter would realize that he was to be the very material out of which the church was to be built. He was not the foundation, the ledge of rock on which the church was to be built. That stone is seen to be Jesus and man's revealed recognition of him as Lord. However, Peter was a "living stone" placed with all other such saved sinners into the body of Christ.

Here is seen a second truth. We in the church need to
know who we are if we are to ring the bell of redemption's
liberty for a lost and dying world. Too many of God's
people have thought themselves spectators at a religious
wrestling match where they pay their tithes and spend their
time listening to and watching the clerical athletes articulate
their opinions and stretch their ecclesiastical muscles. At
the same time, too many pastors and other leaders in the
church have fancied themselves as those paid pros who must
perform feats that bring accolades. Beloved, such is not so.
We are not jesters in a religious court. We are "the sons of
God." We are the church of the Lord Jesus Christ. Jesus
has determined that who he is, we are to be as he lives in
us; and what he has come to do, we are to do as we lift
him up. Who are we? What is the church? We are the extension of the saving life of Christ upon this earth. Let us not
be cowed by criticism nor detoured by the devil's deputies
of deception. We have one identity, that is him. We know
but one calling, the clear commission of evangelistic endeavor.

Yes, when we are sure through the Spirit who Jesus is
and what he is up to, and as we understand our identity with
him so that we walk in step with the stream of his sovereign
strategy, we then will hear the sounds of liberty pealing forth
through our churches to the waiting hearts of hungry men.
This is an affirmation. Jesus said, "I will give unto thee the
keys of the kingdom of heaven: and whatsoever thou shalt
bind on earth shall be bound in heaven." This is our stewardship. Our Lord has assigned to the church the ministry of
reconciliation. He has said that only as we share shall men
hear the tolling of the bells of salvation's liberty, freedom
through the church for all who believe.

How does the church bring freedom? What is the church's ministry in these days of patriotic endeavor? It is not the cheap theatrics of a sideshow carnival or the marvelous antics of Madison Avenue promotion by which the church brings freedom to men. The witness of the church is simply the extension of the kingdom as we share Christ always and everywhere in the normal traffic patterns of our lives. It is by the serious acceptance of the Great Commission's assignment, "Go ye and make disciples, mark them, and mature them," that the church shall offer freedom to men in bondage. It is the acknowledgement of the Great Commission's assurance, "Lo I am with you always and everywhere." When is it that freedom comes through the church? It is when we are letting Christ's freedom ring through our lives in our local congregations while the hosts of Satan flee and the gates of hell shall not hold those from Christ to whom we take the gospel.

Freedom will come in our day as it has come in days gone by, not simply in the shedding of blood by men of patriotic commitment, but sublimely in the sharing of Christ, by the church triumphant through which comes true freedom.